MICHAEL GREEN

THE DAY DEATH DIED

InterVarsity Press
Downers Grove
Illinois 60515

© 1982 by Michael Green

*InterVarsity Press is the book-publishing division of Inter-Varsity Christian
Fellowship, a student movement active on campus at hundreds of universities,
colleges and schools of nursing. For information about local and regional activities,
write IVCF, 233 Langdon St., Madison, WI 53703.*

*Distributed in Canada through InterVarsity Press, 1875 Leslie St.,
Unit 10, Don Mills, Ontario M3B 2M5, Canada.*

Acknowledgment is made to the following for permission to reprint copyrighted material:

*Scripture quotations are from the Revised Standard Version of the Bible,
copyrighted 1946, 1952 © 1971, 1973, by the Division of Christian Education,
National Council of the Churches of Christ in the USA, and used by permission.*

*Lines from "Death" are reprinted by permission of Macmillan Publishing Co., Inc.,
from Collected Poems of W. B. Yeats. Copyright 1933 by Macmillan Publishing
Co., Inc., renewed 1961 by Bertha Georgie Yeats; and by permission of Michael
and Anne Yeats and Macmillan London Limited.*

*Lines from "Do Not Go Gentle into That Good Night" are from Dylan Thomas,
The Collected Poems of Dylan Thomas. Copyright 1952 by Dylan Thomas.
Reprinted by permission of New Directions Publishing Corporation and by
permission of J. M. Dent & Sons, London.*

Cover photograph: Gary Irving

ISBN 0-87784-391-0

Printed in the United States of America

Library of Congress Cataloging in Publication Data

Green, Michael, 1930-
    The day death died.

    Bibliography: p.
    1.   Jesus Christ–Resurrection.   I.   Title.
BT481.G73   232'.5   82-6522
ISBN 0-87784-391-0   AACR2

14	13	12	11	10	9	8	7	6	5	4	3	2	1
93	92	91	90	89	88	87	86	85	84	83	82		

For Jenny

Is It True and Does It Matter?

Christianity is unique among the religions of the world. It is based on the conviction that its founder, Jesus Christ, rose again from the dead on the first Easter day.

Millions of people believe that with all their hearts: I am one of them. Millions more regard it as a pious fairy tale, the sort of thing that brings a crumb of comfort when you stand by an open grave. Millions more have never really thought about it. It has never occurred to them to do so.

I have written this book for all three categories. I want Christians to have a clearer view of the resurrection of Jesus Christ because its impact can transform every aspect of their lives. I want those with a vague faith to see the reality of the resurrection and come face to face with its dynamic power. And I want those who have never really looked into it to realize the solid basis, both in history and experience, for the resurrection of Jesus Christ. I want them to discover him personally.

It is perhaps a good thing—and certainly a convenient thing—that the crux of Christianity rests squarely on this single issue of the resurrection of Christ. It enables us to concentrate on a comparatively small door, but one which could open into a vast room. If Christ rose from the dead, then the implications are enormous. If he did not, then Christianity can be relegated to one of the mystery religions, and Jesus can be set alongside the *avatars* of Hindu mythology.

The resurrection is the cornerstone on which the whole of Christianity, both in its corporate and individual aspects, is built. If it is false, the entire edifice collapses. If it is true, the consequences for our world and for our lives are immense. That is why I set out years ago to write a book examining the evidence for the resurrection and drawing out the implications of that evidence.

The reception accorded to that book, *Man Alive!* and the many reprints and translations it has had, seem to show that the need for such an examination was real. The book is out of date now because the illustrative matter it contains was highly contemporary. But the need remains. People continue to ask two questions of the resurrection story: Is it true? and Does it matter? So I set out to revise *Man Alive!* but decided instead that a fresh book on the same theme would be more useful. Only a small amount of the original material appears in these pages.

The Day Death Died is written to lay before the honest inquirer the evidence upon which Christians confidently assert that Jesus Christ rose from the grave and can be known personally today. And it is written to open the eyes of Christian believers to a new world that began in the light of the first Easter, the day death died.

Is it true?

Does it matter?

If you think these are issues worth pursuing, read on . . .

THE HEART OF THE MATTER

1

■ What is life all about?

■ What is happening to our society, indeed to our world, as it seems to rush toward the brink of disaster, apparently out of control?

■ Is there a life beyond the grave? Or do we go out like a light?

Who has not asked such questions from time to time, before brushing them under the carpet because they are too uncomfortable? But trying to forget them does no good. They refuse to go away.

All the great religions of the world attempt an answer, however tentative, to issues like these. Christianity certainly does. And Christianity is the faith which, above all others, has affected the lives of millions of every color, nationality and social class in the world for over nearly two thousand years. It can make a fair claim to universal appeal and relevance. But what lies at the heart of Christianity?

Is it primarily a matter of belief? Is it a pattern of Sunday church going? Is it a code of conduct which tries to embody love? Or is it, maybe, just a widely diffused addition to the culture of the West?

Christianity is none of these. Of course, Christians do have specific beliefs. They worship God together. They behave in certain ways. And to a greater or lesser extent they affect the climate of the society they live in. But these do not bring us to the heart of the matter.

The Key to Christianity

The key to Christianity is the resurrection of Jesus Christ from the grave. That is the heart of the matter. For Christianity does not claim that Jesus was a good teacher and a fine man. It maintains that in Jesus, God broke into our world. His whole life was a demonstration of what God is like. And when men crucified him through envy and hatred on the first Good Friday, God raised him from the dead on Easter day, vindicating his claims, his teaching, his life and his sacrificial death.

That is, and always has been, the Christian claim. So if you want to examine the truth of Christianity, and whether or not you can credit the answers it gives to the problems of our world, it is to the resurrection you should turn.

14

Professor C. E. M. Joad, a noted broadcaster and philosopher at London University, was once asked whom of all past figures in history he would most like to meet, and what he would most like to ask him. He replied that he would most like to meet Jesus Christ, and he would want to ask him "the most important question in the world: 'Did you or did you not rise from the dead?' "

There was one spot on the battlefield of Waterloo which was taken and retaken three times during that memorable day. Both Napoleon and Wellington saw its vital importance and concentrated their attention upon it. Its final capture by the British troops contributed in large measure to the outcome of the battle. So it is with the resurrection of Jesus Christ. Its significance is crucial for believers and for inquirers alike. The resurrection is essential for Christianity.

This was realized by two young students, West and Lyttleton, in the cynical, pleasure-seeking days of the eighteenth century, when unbelief was as fashionable as it is today. They were friends of Dr. Johnson and the poet Alexander Pope. They were in the swim of society. And they decided to attack Christianity at its very root. So Lyttleton settled down to disprove the conversion of Saul of Tarsus to Christianity, and West to prove that Jesus never rose from the dead. When the two of them met again, they were both somewhat shamefaced. Each had a confession to make. In their study of the evidence they had been forced to unwelcome conclusions. In Lyttleton's case, he had found irrefutable evidence to show that Saul, the famous persecutor of Christians, *had* turned into Paul, the most celebrated missionary the Christian church has ever had. And West had become convinced that Jesus *did* rise from the dead. His book, *Observations on the History and Evidences of the Resurrection of Jesus Christ,* 1747, bears on its flyleaf the significant admonition, "Blame not before thou hast examined the truth."

In our own day, a young journalist was inclined towards the negative conclusions of skeptical theologians. He admired the character of Jesus, but felt his story rested on insecure historical foundations, and that the gospel materials were unreliable and late. He was convinced that miracles did not happen then and do not happen now. But the story of Jesus fascinated him. He determined that when he had time he would look into the matter and write a sensitive and credible account of those last tragic days of Jesus, the final phase of a memorable life. But when he came to study the evidence, he, like Gilbert West, was constrained to write his book on the other side. Frank Morison's *Who Moved the Stone?* has had phenomenal popularity and influence. With great honesty he has entitled the first chapter "The book which refused to be written."

The evidence for the resurrection of Jesus Christ is very strong. I invite you to come with me and examine some of it. For without a doubt it is the linchpin of Christianity. It is the clearest clue we have to the purpose and destiny of life. It *is* the heart of the matter.

Central though it is, the resurrection is a subject that is curiously avoided by many who call themselves Christians. Lord Ismay recalls that when he was Chairman of the B.B.C. only one of the six thousand sermons preached on the air shed any light on this subject.

And I remember visiting a consultant in a London hospital. He was lying in bed, dying of leukemia. A specialist in the disease, he had developed it himself. I was called to see him. And he was angry—not because of his disease, though he was only in his forties—but because of church leaders who speak in such muffled tones about the heart of Christianity. An agnostic for years, he had, lying there in bed, read two books that had brought him to a clear and joyful faith in the risen Christ. And he asked, "Why have I never had the evidence clearly put to me before?"

If It Is True . . .

Consider the issues that hang on the resurrection of Jesus Christ.

If it is true, then we can be sure that God exists. And he is at once seen to be who Jesus proclaimed him to be: one who not only made us but loves us, and cares for us so much that he came to be one of us.

If it is true, then there is a life after death. Jesus, who told us that in his Father's house were many resting places, can be believed. He came back from death and demonstrated the truth of what he had taught.

If it is true, then Jesus Christ really is the Way, the

17

Truth, the Life. No other religion has been able to make, let alone substantiate, a claim that its founder rose from the dead and is alive today. Jesus has every right to be considered *the* bridge between God and man—*if* he rose from the dead.

If it is true, then there is a future for mankind. His resurrection is a first installment of the better world we all want but seem incapable of producing. But as Chancellor Adenauer put it, "If Jesus Christ is not alive, I see no hope for the human race."

If it is true, it puts suffering and death in a new light. It tells us that this life with all its pain and anguish is not the end. On the contrary, this life is a training school for eternity. The first Easter was the day death died.

Those who know the risen Christ will spend eternity with him. He who came to share our precarious life, offers us a share of his eternal life—*if* the resurrection story is true.

A great deal hangs on whether or not Jesus Christ rose from the dead. This is a subject on which nobody can afford to be an agnostic. The stakes are too high. Mercifully, as Lord Darling, formerly Lord Chief Justice of England, once put it, "We, as Christians, are asked to take a very great deal on trust: the teachings, for example, and the miracles of Jesus. If we had to take all on trust, I, for one, should be skeptical. The crux of the problem of whether Jesus was or was not what he proclaimed himself to be must surely depend on the truth or otherwise of the resurrection. On that

18

greatest point we are not merely asked to have faith. In its favor as a living truth there exists such overwhelming evidence, positive and negative, factual and circumstantial, that no intelligent jury in the world could fail to bring in the verdict that the resurrection story is true."

The judge was right in seeing the resurrection as the hinge on which Christianity turns. Was he right in concluding that, incredible though it may seem, it actually happened? That is the question to which we now turn.

CLEARING
THE
GROUND
2

The proper way to approach any supposed event in the past is first of all to lay aside prejudice, secondly to hear the claim, thirdly to assess the evidence on which it rests, and fourthly to examine the presuppositions of those who make it. So let us follow those four steps as we begin to examine the resurrection of Jesus Christ.

Renouncing Prejudice

First, let us try to lay aside prejudice either in favor of the Christian claim or against it.

We are all influenced more than we care to admit by our background, the opinions of our friends, and the assumptions of our culture. Christians have no interest in obscurantism: after all, they follow one whom they claim to be the Truth. If Jesus did not rise from the dead, the sooner Christians stop maintaining he did, the better. There is no excuse for hiding behind tradition or for taking refuge in fairy tales. If the resurrection is false, we should abandon the Christian camp for the humanist.

But there is a lot less of that thoughtless Christian prejudice around than there used to be. It is perhaps more common to find prejudice among those who, for one reason or another, have ignored or rejected the Christian claim.

Apathetic Prejudice

A great many people could not care less. They say, "Well, maybe he did rise from the dead; maybe he didn't. What does it matter?" This apathy, this indifference to truth, seems unfortunately to be on the increase in our society. Perhaps television has something to do with it. We cannot do much to affect the things we see on the screen, so why bother?

Whatever the cause, apathy is totally misguided, and it rests upon a misunderstanding. It is misguided because, as we saw at the end of the last chapter, the resurrection, if true, has the most staggering implications for every single person on this planet, and for the destiny of the human race. And the misunderstanding would seem to be that Jesus was just a man like the rest of us, and if he rose from the grave it is rather as if someone who had drowned in the ocean was resuscitated by a kiss of life after being dragged back to the shore. Of course, the Christian claim is nothing remotely like this. It is that Jesus Christ "being raised from the dead will never die again; death no longer has dominion over him" (Romans 6:9). We are not talking about temporary resuscitation, but resurrection to a new and lasting quality of life.

If it is true, it is exceedingly important. So let us put apathy aside, and see where the evidence leads us.

Theological Prejudice

Theology is also sometimes affected by prejudice. A great deal of modern theology is concerned with "demythologizing" (which often turns out to mean "explaining away") biblical concepts such as the Incarnation or the resurrection of Jesus. We must not, they say, present the Christian faith in such a way that makes it hard for people to believe. We must not stick to the concept of a literal, bodily resurrection. On the contrary, let us concede that the body of Jesus is rotting in some Palestinian grave, but that his spirit (whatever that may mean) lives on. We shall be examining this view in more depth later. Here it is sufficient to notice that it goes back to the eighteenth-century philosopher and theologian Schleiermacher, who wanted to preserve religion from the chill winds of science on the one hand and history on the other. But it is hard to persuade the man in the street that such a procedure is not dishonest. Did Jesus rise or not? That remains the question, and it should certainly be open

23

to the keenest critique of science and historical investigation.

A rather more subtle variety of the same theological prejudice is found in the writings of Rudolf Bultmann and his followers. In deference to the existentialist philosophy prevailing on the continent for much of this century, Bultmann and his colleagues have argued that it is improper to examine "the Easter event." We are not able to get back beyond "the Easter faith." The empty tomb, he rightly maintains, is not nearly so important as the risen presence of Christ. So he abandons faith in the physical resurrection of Jesus, locates his Christian confidence in the confession of the Easter faith by the early church, and construes it as meaning that the cross, which he believes to have been the end of the Jesus story, has saving significance.

Now there are all sorts of influences that have combined to lead Professor Bultmann to write as he does. We are not concerned with them at present. But three questions nevertheless force us to confront the position he has advanced. First, granted the importance of the Easter faith, what was the Easter fact that gave rise to it? Second, if Jesus did not rise from the dead, what sort of sense does it make to say that you have faith in him as living Lord? Third, if history disproves Christianity, then Christianity is false, and it is much better to say so. A number of Bultmann's close disciples have in fact taken this step. Theological prejudice should not be allowed to keep us from examining the evidence of the New Testament. It is no good claiming that modern man will not credit the resurrection, or that its historicity is irrelevant once its symbolic force is granted. In sheer integrity, we must put aside preconceptions and expose ourselves to the sources.

Scientific Prejudice

The third and most widespread form of prejudice on this subject springs from the study of science. The resurrection must be ruled out of court. It is impossible! Such dogmatism is not the normal way for reputable scientists to examine a problem. True, there is an impatience with miracles in many scientific circles, but it is matched by an increasing recognition of the limitations of our knowledge and the mystery of the universe.

There are just two points that need to be made with regard to science and the resurrection. The first concerns scientific method. This is unashamedly inductive. That is to say, it begins with the phenomena and then seeks to arrive at generalizations that account for them. It does not begin by ruling out of order facts that are inconvenient. Instead, it examines them. And most of the advances in scientific enquiry have taken place when scientists have wrestled with the one awkward fact that did not fit into the prevailing theory. In principle there is no scientific reason why Jesus could not have risen from the grave.

The second point that needs to be made is this: we are not claiming that there is a certain class of people that get up out of their coffins. The first-century writers weren't claiming this either.

What we are maintaining is that Jesus was no ordinary man. We believe that in this very special person, one who was more than man, the forces of death met their match. We believe that there are good reasons for supposing that Jesus was no less God than man. How then can we be sure that he could not overcome death? He lived a uniquely unsullied life, perfect at every point. How can we be certain a life that had given no foothold to sin could not master death? We have no other example of the "sinless" category to compare him with. Jesus made the whole of his credibility rest upon the assertion that he would "do a Jonah" on his contemporaries; and just as Jonah came back from his three-day "death" inside the great fish, so Jesus himself would come back from the jaws of death (Matthew 12:39-41).

So let us lay aside the dogmatic prejudice that asserts "It could never happen" and see if, according to all the available evidence, it *did* happen in this one solitary case of Jesus. If he was perfect man, if he was more than man, we cannot rule it out of court.

Having attempted to recognize and divest ourselves of prejudice, let us hear the Christian claim about Jesus. Just what were his contemporaries laying claim to?

Hearing the Claim
Here is the earliest evidence in the New Testament, presented by Paul the apostle in the mid-fifties of the

first century, just twenty years after the event:

For I delivered to you as of first importance what I also received, that Christ died for our sins in accordance with the scriptures, that he was buried, that he was raised on the third day in accordance with the scriptures, and that he appeared to Cephas, then to the twelve. Then he appeared to more than five hundred brethren at one time, most of whom are still alive, though some have fallen asleep. Then he appeared to James, then to all the apostles. Last of all, as to one untimely born, he appeared also to me. For I am the least of the apostles, unfit to be called an apostle, because I persecuted the church of God. But by the grace of God I am what I am, and his grace toward me was not in vain. . . . Whether then it was I or they, so we preach and so you believed.

Now if Christ is preached as raised from the dead, how can some of you say that there is no resurrection of the dead? But if there is no resurrection of the dead, then Christ has not been raised; if Christ has not been raised, then our preaching is in vain and your faith is in vain. We are even found to be misrepresenting God, because we testified of God that he raised Christ, whom he did not raise if it is true that the dead are not raised. For if the dead are not raised, then Christ has not been raised. If Christ has not been raised, your faith is futile and you are still in your sins. Then those also who have fallen asleep in Christ have perished. If for this life only we have hoped in Christ, we are of all men most to be pitied.

But in fact Christ has been raised from the dead, the first fruits of those who have fallen asleep. (1 Corinthians 15:3-20)

This passage is of the utmost value. It shows how fundamental the resurrection was to Paul, to the Jerusalem apostles, and to the Christians in Corinth as well. It was clearly at the very heart of the faith.

Ten years later we find Peter taking up his pen and exclaiming,

Blessed be the God and Father of our Lord Jesus Christ! By his great mercy we have been born anew to a living hope through the resurrection of Jesus Christ from the dead, and to an inheritance which is imperishable, undefiled, and unfading, kept in heaven for you, who by God's power are guarded through faith for a salvation ready to be revealed in the last time. (1 Peter 1:3-5)

Those to whom this letter was addressed were in imminent danger of a summary trial and agonizing death for their faith: hundreds of Christians were burned alive in Nero's persecution of A.D. 64, a situation which may well be reflected in this letter. So Peter continues:

In this you rejoice, though now for a little while you may have to suffer various trials, so that the genuineness of your faith, more precious than gold which though perishable is tested by fire, may redound to praise and glory and honor at the revelation of Jesus Christ. Without having seen him you love him; though you do not now see him you believe in him and rejoice with unutterable and exalted joy. (1 Peter 1:6-8)

A few verses later he burst out:

Through him you have confidence in God, who raised him from the dead and gave him glory, so that your faith and hope are in God. (1 Peter 1:21)

There can be no doubt that the resurrection was of crucial importance for both the writer and the recipients of this letter.

The letter to Hebrew Christians was probably written about A.D. 68 and calls "the resurrection of the dead" one of the "elementary doctrines" of the Christian faith, so cardinal is it, and so universally believed in the Christian church. This remarkable letter concentrates our gaze on Jesus as the eternal high priest, reconciling man and God in a way no other priesthood has ever been able to do.

The former priests were many in number, because they were prevented by death from continuing in office; but he holds his priesthood permanently, because he continues for ever. Consequently he is able for all time to save those who draw near to God through him, since he always lives to make intercession for them. (Hebrews 7:23-25)

Or again

When Christ had offered for all time a single sacrifice for sins, he sat down at the right hand of God, then to wait until his enemies should be made a stool for his feet. (Hebrews 10:12-13)

Mark is usually considered the earliest of the Gospels, and it was probably written by the mid-sixties of the first century A.D. Mark records three predictions by Jesus of what is going to befall him. They come in 8:31, 9:31 and 10:33-34. They all envisage a bloody, treacherous death for Jesus, and they all indicate he will rise again on the third day. Mark's actual account of what took place at Easter is instructive:

> And when the sabbath was past, Mary Magdalene, and Mary the mother of James, and Salome, bought spices, so that they might go and anoint him. And very early on the first day of the week they went to the tomb when the sun had risen. And they were saying to one another, "Who will roll away the stone for us from the door of the tomb?" And looking up, they saw that the stone was rolled back—it was very large. And entering the tomb, they saw a young man sitting on the right side, dressed in a white robe; and they were amazed. And he said to them, "Do not be amazed; you seek Jesus of Nazareth, who was crucified. He has risen, he is not here; see the place where they laid him. But go, tell his disciples and Peter that he is going before you to Galilee; there you will see him, as he told you." And they went out and fled from the tomb; for trembling and astonishment had come upon them; and they said nothing to any one, for they were afraid. (Mark 16:1-8)

With these remarkable words Mark's Gospel comes to

an abrupt end. Perhaps he intended it to end there, with awe and amazement before the ultimate act of God in raising Christ from the grave. Perhaps he was arrested or otherwise prevented from completing the Gospel. In any event, the original text finished there, and in the second century three alternative versions competed for the honor of bringing the Gospel to an end.

It is widely held that Matthew's Gospel was written in the eighties, while Luke's Gospel and the Acts of the Apostles are variously dated in the sixties or eighties. There is a great deal about the resurrection in all three.

Matthew tells us that as the women left the tomb with fear and great joy and ran to tell the disciples,

Jesus met them and said, "Hail!" And they came up and took hold of his feet and worshiped him. Then Jesus said to them, "Do not be afraid; go and tell my brethren to go to Galilee, and there they will see me." . . . Now the eleven disciples went to Galilee, to the mountain to which Jesus had directed them. And when they saw him they worshiped him; but some doubted. And Jesus came and said to them, "All authority in heaven and on earth has been given to me. Go therefore and make disciples of all nations, baptizing them in the name of the Father and of the Son and of the Holy Spirit, teaching them to observe all that I have commanded you; and lo, I am with you always, to the close of the age." (Matthew 28:9-10, 16-20)

With those words Matthew brings his Gospel to an end.

Luke's account is too long to quote here. It comes in chapter 24 of his Gospel and, after telling of the empty tomb and the women, goes on to recount the matchless story of two disciples, discouraged and fed up, walking to Emmaus on Easter afternoon. Jesus joins them, but they do not recognize him until he excites them by explaining the Scriptures to them, and reveals himself to them in the way he breaks bread at table. Amazed and thrilled, they return to Jerusalem by night, and find the disciples saying, "The Lord has risen indeed, and has appeared to Simon!" What happened at that interview with Simon, Luke does not record. But he does tell of various meetings of the risen Christ with his disciples, before he leaves them for the last time and returns to his Father in heaven.

The Acts of the Apostles are full of references to the resurrection. This book was written to take the story of Jesus into its second stage, as his disciples began to spread all over the ancient world the account of the amazing person they had been privileged to know, and the achievements of his life, death and resurrection. The resurrection and ascension of Jesus are summarized in the first paragraph of the book, and then one of the qualifications of a replacement for the traitor Judas is laid down: he must be "with us a witness to his resurrection" (Acts 1:22).

The whole of the rest of the book is concerned with this witness to the resurrection, which was the prime differentiating mark of the early Christians. Apart from that they were hardly distinguishable from other Jews. But they had the effrontery to maintain that Jesus, whom their rulers had condemned and whom the Romans had executed, was the Son of God, and that God had raised him from the tomb. This was insurrection indeed. So they were opposed, imprisoned, tortured and killed for the message that had brought their movement into being.

The story begins in Jerusalem with their forthright preaching on the Day of Pentecost:

Men of Israel, hear these words: Jesus of Nazareth, a man attested to you by God with mighty works and wonders and signs which God did through him in your midst, as you yourselves know—this Jesus, delivered up according to the definite plan and foreknowledge of God, you crucified and killed by the hands of lawless men. But God raised him up, having loosed the pangs of death, because it was not possible for him to be held by it. . . . This Jesus God raised up, and of that we all are witnesses. (Acts 2:22-24, 32)

There is a great deal more in this vein. Luke's summary of the spread of the gospel in that first Jerusalem community is as follows:

And with great power the apostles gave their testimony to the resurrection of the Lord Jesus, and great grace was upon them all. (Acts 4:33)

Three other examples from the later parts of the book make the prime importance of the resurrection obvious. At Athens, Paul so concentrated on *Iesous kai anastasis* (Jesus and resurrection) that they thought he was announcing a couple of new deities (Acts 17:18)! Again, Paul in prison and making his defense before the Roman governor, Felix, can say, "With respect to the resurrection of the dead I am on trial before you this day" (Acts 24:21). Once more he makes the issue abundantly clear in his trial before King Agrippa:

> I stand here testifying both to small and great, saying nothing but what the prophets and Moses said would come to pass: that the Christ must suffer, and that, by being the first to rise from the dead, he would proclaim light both to the people and to the Gentiles. (Acts 26:22-23)

Our survey of the New Testament evidence is almost complete. We ought, however, to glance at the Gospel of John and the Revelation of John, both of which were probably completed in the nineties of the first century. The Gospel tells how Jesus appeared to Mary Magdalene, to the twelve, to Thomas and to Peter and John. It is a marvelous piece of writing. It breathes authenticity. Read the last two chapters of St. John's Gospel for yourself and feel the force of them. Could they have been written by a deranged mind? Could they have been written to deceive? And notice that these two chapters do not come from the author of the Gospel in isolation. He speaks for the Christian community he belongs to, and that community puts its hand to what he writes:

This is the disciple who is bearing witness to these

things, and who has written these things; and we *know* that his testimony is true. (John 21:24)

As for the book of Revelation, the whole theme hinges on the proposition that "the Lamb once slain is in the midst of the throne of God." It claims that in the death and resurrection of Jesus we have the clue to the meaning of history and the destiny of man. Because of the resurrection we can face the utmost in catastrophe confident that "the Lord God omnipotent is reigning." Nowhere does the basic claim come through more clearly than in Revelation 1:17-18 where John has a vision of the living Christ:

> When I saw him, I fell at his feet as though dead. But he laid his right hand upon me, saying, "Fear not, I am the first and the last, and the living one; I died, and behold I am alive for evermore, and I have the keys of Death and Hades."

Assessing the Evidence

Such, in brief, is the evidence from the New Testament. How shall we assess it?

First, I am struck by the breadth of this testimony. It is brought before us in every strand of the material: Matthew, Mark, Luke, John, all have independent elements within them, derived from different eyewitnesses. The resurrection plays an equally important part in the writings of Peter and Paul, and in Hebrews and Revelation. If it is not true, then the whole of the New Testament would need to be rewritten.

Secondly, I am impressed by the harmony of this

material. It is by no means copied from one writer by another. There are what appear to be minor discrepancies: Mark speaks of one young man (angel?) at the tomb, Luke of two. The writers are clearly struggling to describe the indescribable. They allude to the doubt that struck the disciples before it turned into joy. They were not easy bait for a fraud.

Thirdly, the antiquity of this testimony is impressive. It is written between twenty and sixty years after the event, all the different strands of it. And that is very early by ancient reckoning.

Tacitus is the main Roman historian of the Empire in the time of Jesus. He wrote some eighty years after most of the events he described, yet his accuracy is rated very highly. The other major historian of this period, Suetonius, wrote a century after the events he described. Within Judaism itself, the First Book of Maccabees was written about 100 B.C. and tells of the exploits of the freedom fighters seventy years earlier. This does not prevent its being considered a most reliable document.

Why, then, should we discredit the Gospel records (when the gap between event and writing is much shorter, and the attestation much broader) simply because Jesus was not an ordinary person and the events of his life and death were not ordinary events? The famous scientist, Ambrose Fleming, makes this point well:

We must ask ourselves whether it is probable that such a book, describing events that occurred about

thirty or forty years previously, could have been
accepted and cherished if the stories of abnormal
events in it were false or mythical. It is impossible,
because the memory of all elderly persons regard-
ing the events of history thirty or forty years before
is perfectly clear. No one could now issue a biog-
raphy of Queen Victoria, who died thirty-one years
ago, full of anecdotes which were quite untrue.
They would be contradicted at once. They would
certainly not be generally accepted and passed on
as true. Hence there is great improbability that the
account of the resurrection given by the gospels
is a pure invention. This mythical theory has had
to be abandoned because it will not bear close scru-
tiny.

Is there any external support for the resurrection of
Jesus Christ? There is, both in Roman and Jewish
sources, and perhaps in archaeology.

Tacitus, describing the Fire of Rome in A.D. 64,
tells how Christians were made scapegoats by the Emperor Nero for this blaze:

The name Christian comes to them from Christ,
who was executed in the reign of Tiberius by the
procurator Pontius Pilate; and the pernicious su-
perstition, suppressed for a while, broke out afresh
and spread, not only through Judea, the source
of the malady, but even throughout Rome itself,
where everything vile is feted. (*Annals* 15.44)

Tacitus was writing about A.D. 112. At the same time
Pliny, governor of Bithynia, was asking the Emperor

Trajan what he should do about the growth of Christians in his area, whose monotheism was threatening the sale of sacrificial animals, the survival of the temples and the prestige of the emperor. He said that the Christians lived exemplary lives but refused to worship the images of the gods. Rather, they met on a certain fixed day (Sunday, the day on which Christians claimed the resurrection took place) and sang in alternate verses a hymn "to Christ as God" (*Epistles*, 10.96).

Josephus, the Jewish general turned historian, wrote about the turn of the century. His work contains a remarkable passage about Jesus which is worth quoting in full:

> And there arose about this time Jesus, a wise man, if indeed we should call him a man; for he was a doer of marvelous deeds, a teacher of men who receive the truth with pleasure. He won over many Jews and also many Greeks. This man was the Messiah. And when Pilate had condemned him to the cross at the instigation of our own leaders, those who had loved him did not at once cease. For he appeared to them the third day alive again, as the holy prophets had predicted, and said many other wonderful things about him. And even now the race of Christians, so called after him, has not yet died out. (*Antiquities*, 18.3.3)

This remarkable passage has attracted a lot of attention. Many scholars cannot believe it was written by Josephus. There may be some Christian interpolation here, though it is hard to imagine Christians being so restrained! Moreover, the manuscript tradition is uniform in attributing this passage to Josephus himself. Some of the paragraph is undoubtedly sarcastic: Josephus was no Christian. "If indeed we should call him a man" may be an allusion to his divine claims, and "this man was the Messiah" may refer to the charge affixed to his cross, while the passage about the resurrection may merely reflect Christian preaching. Nevertheless, we have here a remarkable independent testimony to the person, death, resurrection and continuing influence of Jesus among Jews at the end of the first century.

The archaeological evidence is, from the very nature of the case, incapable of being more than circumstantial. But still it is intriguing. It indicates that both the account of Jesus' death and rumors of his resurrection were known to the Roman authorities very early indeed, and that they took swift remedial action.

A remarkable inscription has turned up, belonging to the reign of either Tiberius (A.D. 14-38) or Claudius (A.D. 41-54). In it the emperor expresses his displeasure at reports he has heard of the removal of dead bodies from the tomb, and he warns that he will punish, by the unusual expedient of the death penalty, any further tampering with graves. This inscription was found in Nazareth, the birthplace of Jesus. Pilate must have reported about Jesus to the emperor in Rome. As a matter of fact, Tertullian, a Christian lawyer in the second century, claimed that Pilate's report was still extant in the imperial archives. Presumably Pilate would have taken the line (alluded to in Matthew 28:11-15) that the disciples came and stole the body of Jesus while the soldiers who were supposed to be guarding the tomb had fallen asleep. This would be quite enough to account for the sharp imperial rejoinder!

Examining the Presuppositions

Such is the attestation for the resurrection of Jesus from a whole breadth of Christian sources, together with Roman, Jewish and archaeological support. What are we to make of this evidence? What were the expectations of those first Christians?

Is it simply a case of their being poor, uncritical folk, unable to tell a ghost or a vision from a resurrected friend? I think not. Resurrections were no more common in the first century then they are now. The first disciples were no mere simpletons, easily taken in. Had they been, they would have made few converts in the sophisticated society of the Greco-Roman world, and fewer still among their fellow Jews.

Were they, then, wicked deceivers, determined to get a following for themselves? That is equally incredible. For one thing, you do not allow yourself to be torn limb from limb for a fraud. Had the early Christians been deceivers, some of them would have given way under torture.

Moreover they would not have left so many loose

ends in their story. It is no easier to harmonize all the
details of the resurrection accounts than it is to reconcile accounts of the same event in eight different news-
papers. But had the early Christians been making it
all up they would have made sure that their stories
tallied. They would have ensured that the appearances
were either all of a spiritual Jesus or of a resuscitated,
tangible Jesus, not a curious mixture of the two. No,
the artless lack of collusion, the absence of contrived
agreement in these stories militates against their being
fabrication. These stories were not made up.

Very well then, were the early Christians resorting
to wish-fulfillment? Were they so anxious to see the
resurrection of their friend and master that they came
to believe it had happened?

The trouble with such a view is that there is no evidence whatever to support it. On the contrary, the
accounts indicate that the disciples had no expectation
that Jesus would return from the grave. He had said
he would, but frankly, they did not believe him. When
they were confronted by the events of Easter day, they
were dumbfounded and at first refused to believe it.

And as for the preposterous notion, presented by
some theologians (who should know better), that they
made it all up from a random collection of Old Testament texts and expectations, this is even further
from the truth. As Jews they certainly looked for resurrection. It had been *implicit* in their faith from the
days of Abraham onward. Did not God reveal himself,
saying, "I am (not *I was*) the God of Abraham, Isaac

41

and Jacob"? This faith in the resurrection had been *explicit* at least since the book of Daniel was written (Daniel 12:2). But it was always associated with the end time, the climax of history. Martha, the woman whose brother, Lazarus, Jesus was about to resuscitate, expressed Jewish orthodoxy precisely in her reply to Jesus. "Your brother will rise again," Jesus had said. Martha said to him, "I know that he will rise again in the resurrection at the last day" (John 11:23-24).

No, the disciples had no expectation that Jesus would rise from the dead before that last day, and they certainly did not dream up his resurrection out of texts from the Old Testament. There are remarkably few such texts and they all refer to the final resurrection of the just at the end of the world, not to God's vindication of his Messiah in their own lifetime.

One more question before we turn, in the next chapter, to examine the evidence which persuaded these Jews that their Jesus was alive again, and for ever.

Can we reconcile their testimony to the risen Jesus with a purely spiritual resurrection? Could they have meant that the body of Jesus stayed in the tomb but that his spirit lived on—a sort of "John Brown's body lies a-mouldering in the grave, but his soul goes marching on"? Once again, the answer must be negative, and that for a variety of reasons.

In the first place it is very hard to see what is meant by a spiritual resurrection. How would it be different from happy memories of the departed or his continuing influence?

Secondly, a spiritual resurrection would make nonsense of the claim explicitly referred to in most of the accounts we have looked at, that the resurrection took place *on the third day.*

Thirdly, it would leave untouched the problem of what happened to the corpse, or why the tomb never became a place of pilgrimage.

Fourthly, a spiritual resurrection in A.D. 30 is totally at odds with the convictions of Judaism that people would have a physical resurrection at the last day. Wherever resurrection is referred to in Judaism, there is a firm belief in the *resurrection of the body.* This comes in Old Testament passages like Ezekiel 37, and in the Jewish writings which came after the Old Testament was complete, such as Judith 16:17, 2 Baruch 49:2—50:4, Sibylline Oracles 4.179-182. Physical resurrection was the unvarying hope of the Jews. The Pharisees held to it strongly. It is incredible that the disciples would have been trained in any other view. Moreover, as we have seen in 1 Corinthians 15, Paul is at pains to show that Jesus was *buried,* and that it was as one dead and buried that he rose again on the third day (15:4). The whole thrust of this chapter is directed not against materialists who thought that this life was all there is, but against Greeks who believed in the immortality of the soul. Paul does not say to them "Right, have it your way. Resurrection is just my way of talking about the immortality of the soul, which you believe." He tells them that if they do not believe in the resurrection of Jesus their faith is vain, their salvation is at risk, their dead are lost, and they are of all men most to be pitied.

We may safely conclude, therefore, that the early Christians were not simpletons or deceivers, that they were not indulging in fantasies of wish-fulfillment or extrapolations from obscure Old Testament texts. They were not maintaining the doctrine of the immortality of the soul.

They were making a claim unique in the history of the world. They were saying that in Jesus the forces of death had met their match. Easter was, in a profound sense, the day death died. The grave had not been able to hold the prince of life. In the next chapter we shall look more closely at the evidence for this most remarkable of claims, one which singles out Christianity from every other faith in the world.

EXAMINING
THE
EVIDENCE
3

There is good evidence for the resurrection of Jesus Christ from the dead. "It is not too much to say," wrote Bishop Westcott, one of the greatest New Testament scholars England has ever produced, "that there is no single historical incident better or more variously attested than the resurrection of Christ." And Sir Edward Clarke, a High Court judge, gives an interesting perspective on the matter when he writes:

As a lawyer I have made a prolonged study of the evidence for the events of Easter Day. To me the evidence is conclusive, and over and over again in the High Court I have secured the verdict on evidence not nearly so compelling. As a lawyer I accept the Gospel evidence unreservedly as the testimony of truthful men to facts that they were able to substantiate.

Or take Thomas Arnold, headmaster of Rugby, who was once Professor of History at Oxford. He put it like this:

> I have been used for many years to study the history of other times, and to examine and weigh the evidence of those who have written about them; and I know of no fact in the history of mankind which is proved by better and fuller evidence of every sort, to the understanding of a fair inquirer, that the great sign that God has given us, that Christ died and rose again from the dead.

These three men, a lawyer, a secular historian and a New Testament scholar, agree that the evidence is overwhelming. What brought them to this conclusion?

The judicial murder of Jesus of Nazareth is not a pleasant story. He was put to death with the connivance of the religious and secular authorities and the backing of public opinion. After a sleepless night, in which he was given no food, endured the mockery of two trials, and had his back lacerated with the cruel Roman cat-o'-nine-tails, he was crucified—an excruciatingly painful death in which every nerve in his body screamed with anguish.

Jesus Was Dead
He died in an unusually quick amount of time, six hours or so. The four executioners came to examine

him before a friend, Joseph of Arimathea, was allowed to take away the body for burial.

These soldiers were experienced at their grisly task: crucifixions were not uncommon in Palestine. They knew a dead man when they saw one—and their commanding officer had heard the condemned man's death-cry himself and was prepared to certify the death to the governor, Pontius Pilate. But just to make sure, they pierced his heart through with a spear. And then a very remarkable thing happened.

We are told on eyewitness authority that "blood and water" came out of the pierced side of Jesus (John 19:34-35). The eyewitness clearly attached great importance to this. Had Jesus still been alive when the spear pierced his side, strong spurts of blood would have emerged with every heartbeat. Instead, the observer noticed semi-solid dark red clots seeping out, distinct and separate from the accompanying watery serum. This is evidence of massive clotting of the blood in the main arteries and is exceptionally strong medical proof of death. It is all the more impressive because John could not possibly have realized its significance to a pathologist.

The "blood and water" from the spear-thrust is proof positive that Jesus was already dead.

Jesus Was Buried

After his death was certified, Jesus was taken down from the cross and buried in a rock tomb nearby. The tomb belonged to a hitherto secret disciple, Joseph of

Arimathea. The body was placed on a stone ledge, wound tightly in strips of cloth, and covered with spices. John's Gospel tells us some seventy-five pounds were used, and that is likely enough. Joseph was a rich man, and no doubt wanted to make up for his cowardice during the lifetime of Jesus by giving him a splendid burial. The amount, though great, has parallels. Rabbi Gamaliel, a contemporary of Jesus, was buried with eighty pounds of spice when he died.

But details like this make nonsense of the theory that Jesus was not really dead, and that, revived in the cool of the tomb, he crept out and persuaded his gullible disciples that he was risen from the dead.

This rationalistic refuge from the strong evidence for the resurrection has a long ancestry. It was produced by Schleiermacher in 1799 and was revived in the 1960s by Hugh Schonfield in *The Passover Plot*. It ignores the deadly character of Jesus' wounds, the careful examination by experienced Roman executioners, the blood and water, the constricting graveclothes, the crushing weight of spices, the lack of human help, and the sealed tomb.

What is more, it is psychologically impossible. How could someone who crept half dead out of a tomb, needing bandaging, strengthening, and every care, have persuaded his followers that he was the Lord of life and conqueror of death?

Granted, then, the death and burial of Jesus, what solid grounds are there for supposing that he rose from the dead?

1. The Empty Tomb

As we have seen in the records we looked at in the last chapter, the women who came to pay their last respects to Jesus on the first Easter morning by anointing his body (omitted in the haste of his burial before sundown on Friday) were shattered to find that his body had gone.

It is difficult to deny that the tomb of Jesus was empty on the first Easter day—unless we resort to the historical oddity, suggested by Kirsopp Lake, that they went to the wrong tomb! Did Joseph not know his own tomb? Would the authorities not speedily have exhumed Jesus if his body had been there to find? Would the whole Christian movement have gotten under way on the basis of a wrong identification of tombs in the half-light of Easter morning? No, skepticism must do better than that if it is to win adherents.

The tomb was empty, and this was common ground between friend and foe alike. What the Jews did was not to deny that the tomb was empty, but to offer a natural explanation for the fact. "His disciples came by night and stole him away" (Matthew 28:12-15). Could the fact that the tomb was empty have any more confirmation than that?

It is sometimes said that our earliest witness, Paul, writing twenty years after the event, knows nothing of the empty tomb. His testimony is certainly of the utmost importance. If he knew nothing of the empty tomb we might have to be rather cautious in asserting it. But glance back at his words quoted on pages 27-28.

49

Does it seem to you that he is talking about a vague spiritual survival rather than something palpable and dateable: a resurrection?

First Corinthians 15 is a truly remarkable piece of writing. It comes from one who was a chief opponent of the Christian cause until he was himself turned round in mid-career by the resurrection. The message of the resurrection that he stresses in this passage is something he considers "as of first importance." It is the very heart of Christianity.

Notice that he is not informing the Corinthians of something they did not know, but reminding them of something they heard and accepted at their conversion. That tradition (for such is the meaning, both in Hebrew and Greek, of "I delivered to you," "I received") derives from the very people who had been there, the Jerusalem Christians (see verse 11). He particularly singles out Peter (with his old Aramaic name, "Cephas," in verse 5) and James (the brother of Jesus, who was converted through the resurrection, verse 7).

Not only does the tradition Paul refers to in this passage come from the very core of earliest believers, but it goes back to within a few years of the resurrection itself. Paul says that he "received" this message (verse 3). When? Naturally, at his conversion on the Damascus Road, confirmed by subsequent discussions with the Jerusalem leadership. Paul could not have been converted later than A.D. 35. So what he gives us here is bedrock Christian belief which was already "tradition" in Christian circles by the time Paul became

a Christian, a few years after the events themselves!
It is impossible to exaggerate the importance of 1 Corinthians 15.

Does Paul know anything of the empty tomb?

To be sure, he does not explicitly mention the
empty tomb here. After all, he is not informing them,
but reminding them! But he certainly knew it, and
there are various allusions to it in this passage.

First, he says Jesus was raised *on the third day*. What
does that mean? Surely (as in Acts 10:40), that on the
third day the tomb of Jesus was found to be empty
and Jesus was found to be alive.

Secondly, what would have been the point of saying
"he was buried . . . he was raised" (verse 4) unless Paul
was alluding to the empty tomb? He is asserting that
Jesus was raised from burial.

Thirdly, he makes considerable mention in this
chapter of the parallel between Christ's resurrection
body and the body God will give to Christians in the
resurrection (verses 12-13, 16, 20-23, 35-49). We know
from his second letter to the Christians in Corinth
that Paul did not think of our resurrection in non-
bodily terms (2 Corinthians 5:1-4). He maintains that
just as the physical body of Jesus was transformed at
his resurrection, so it will be with the Christians at the
last day. This analogy would have been utterly impossible for Paul had he not believed that the body of Jesus
was raised from death. The very way he spoke about
the body in resurrection shows that he knew about the
empty tomb.

And remember that "resurrection" meant bodily resurrection to Paul as it would have to any other Pharisee. You can search the rabbinic writings in vain to find any mention of a "spiritual resurrection." Often, indeed, they spoke of it in terms so crass that the New Testament writers have to protest against this element in their background and speak of a "spiritual body." But a body it remains.

There can be no doubt, then, that Paul knew the tradition of the empty tomb and accepted it without bothering to discuss it at length. Like the other Christians, he was much more interested in the risen Jesus than in his empty tomb. Professor Sir Norman Anderson makes this point in an interesting and acute way:

Have you noticed that the references to the empty tomb all come in the Gospels which were written to give the Christian community the facts they wanted to know? In the public preaching to those who were not believers, as recorded in the Acts of the Apostles, there is an enormous emphasis on the fact of the resurrection but not a single reference to the empty tomb. Now, why? To me there is only one answer. There was no point in arguing about the empty tomb. Everyone, friend and opponent, knew that it was empty. The only questions worth arguing about were why it was empty and what its emptiness proved.

Well, what did its emptiness prove? And why was it empty that first Easter day? Suppose the body of Jesus was not raised by God, but removed by men. Who would have wanted to do such a thing? There are only two lots of people to consider: his enemies, who crucified him, or his friends, who loved him—nobody else. The trouble is that neither of these two parties were in the least likely to have done anything of the sort.

The disciples are the most obvious suspects. But the longer you think about it the less plausible it seems. And for two reasons: they could not have done it if they had wanted to, and they would not have done it if they had been able to.

They could not have removed the body of Jesus for the simple reason that there was a guard on the tomb. It is fashionable to disregard the account of the guard on the grounds that it is only recorded in Matthew's Gospel, and in any case looks like Christian propaganda. To my mind, however, it rings true. It is attested, incidentally, by two of the apocryphal Gospels of the second century, and by intelligent Christian writers such as the philosopher Justin and the lawyer Tertullian, also in the second century. Furthermore, it is just what you might expect to happen given the mixture of law and intrigue that went to make up the administration of the province of Judea.

The body of a condemned criminal remained Roman property. That is why Joseph had to go and ask no less a person than the governor for it. As soon as Pilate said "Yes" the whole situation changed. The body was now back in Jewish custody. Responsibility for any riots that might ensue would fall fairly and squarely upon Jewish shoulders.

That is what made the chief priests muster enough courage to brave the governor again, although they knew he was in a black mood, in order to try to persuade him to furnish them with a guard. They were playing the age-old game of passing the buck. But Pilate refused to be drawn. "You have a guard of soldiers; go, make it as secure as you can" (Matthew 27:65). They had indeed: the temple police. Their plan to evade responsibility had failed. Ruefully they set their own guard, having failed to get his! But this did not prevent the tomb being empty on the third day.

So afterward, the priests had to produce the lame story of the watchmen sleeping on duty while the Christians made off with the corpse. Not very good for morale, but better than admitting the resurrection!

How anyone could suppose this story arose in Christian circles for apologetic reasons has always amazed me. The resurrection of Jesus needed no such bolstering to these early disciples. They were far too sure of the reality of the risen Lord in their midst to go around inventing stories of how his tomb came to be empty.

In any case, there are two telltale words in the account that settle the matter—*hēmōn koimōmenōn*, "while we were asleep" (Matthew 28:13). No Christian could have made that up and put it in the mouth of the guards. For if the guards had been sleeping, how could they have known what the Christians were up to? No, the story would only have been of use in Christian propaganda *if the guards had stayed awake!*

The only conceivable reason, therefore, for the circulation of the story about a guard being set on the tomb was that it was true. There had been a guard. It had not prevented the resurrection. And it is eminently credible that the guard was bribed by the Jewish authorities to say that the disciples came and stole the body while they slept. The authorities were simply making the best of a bad situation. The guard on the sealed tomb, complete with a massive millstone at the door, make it very difficult to suppose that the friends of Jesus could possibly have removed the corpse.

And anyway, would they have wanted to? All the records show that they did not expect Jesus to rise from the dead. They were utterly disheartened. They had backed a loser and all they wanted to do was to run away and hide and forget all about the fiasco. Resurrection seems never to have entered their heads.

But even if it were possible to credit these eleven men with such cunning at the moment of their greatest humiliation, what are we to make of the sequel? They were soon joyfully proclaiming the resurrection all over the world, and nothing could stop them. Prison, torture and death proved totally inadequate to change their conviction that Jesus was alive. No, the theory that the disciples stole the body of Jesus is psychologically untenable. They could not if they would, and they would not if they could.

It is no less incredible to suppose that the enemies of Jesus removed his body. At long last they had him where they wanted him. Let him stay there! Would the chief priests, who went to all the trouble of organizing a guard over the tomb, have been so incredibly stupid as to suggest the idea of the resurrection by removing the body? And if, by some quirk of illogicality, they had been so stupid, they would have had no problem in producing the body once the disciples started preaching the resurrection—less than six weeks after the execution! Instead, all they could do was to order the Christians to be silent, and imprison or execute them when they refused to. We can be absolutely sure that the enemies of Jesus did not remove his corpse from the tomb.

Before we leave the question of the tomb, give a thought to the graveclothes. We are told that the graveclothes were left behind in the tomb. One wonders why, if the body was pilfered by friend or enemy. But there is more to it than that. There is an eyewitness account in John's Gospel that says of Peter and John: "Simon Peter came, following him, and went into the tomb; he saw the linen cloths lying, and the napkin, which had been on his head, not lying with the linen cloths but rolled up in a place by itself . . . and he [John] saw and believed" (John 20:6-8).

Why should this fact have made such an impression on John? For this reason. The wrappings were like a chrysalis case when the butterfly has emerged: undisturbed, but empty. Those tightly wound bandages had encased Jesus as closely as the chrysalis case fits round the pupa. The turban round his head would, of course, have been separate from the wrappings round his body. But, like the graveclothes, it retained the shape it had when wound around the head of Jesus.

That is what made such a profound impression on John. It almost seemed as though the body of Jesus had vaporized and passed through the graveclothes. Those that had covered his body were intact, apart from being crushed by the weight of spices. The turban kept its original shape.

What could account for such a strange phenomenon? No grave robber would have been able to enact so remarkable a theft. He would simply have taken the body, graveclothes and all. Had Jesus merely been resuscitated, he would presumably have used the clothes or laid them aside. But as it was, all the signs point to Jesus' having been raised to a new order of life, a new sphere of existence. And he left the graveclothes behind as the butterfly emerging to a new dimension of life leaves behind the cocoon. That sight convinced Peter and John. How about you?

It is even possible that these graveclothes actually survive, in the shroud of Turin. That shroud has really undergone extensive forensic tests. The date is about right, and tiny pollen fragments indicate that it came from the Middle East. But the most remarkable thing about it is that it bears the *negative image* of a crucified man's wounds; and there are, in the cloth, evidences of heat consonant with a transmutation of the body of Jesus to a new dimension of life. I want to be cautious in putting much weight on the shroud, but scholarly opinion is increasingly moving toward believing it to be genuine. I do not mind whether it is or not. In itself it cannot lead anyone to the risen Christ. But it may well be, like the empty tomb and the arrangement of the graveclothes, one more silent witness to the central event, the resurrection of Jesus Christ from the dead.

2. The Resurrection Appearances

The empty tomb alone would never have brought about widespread belief in the resurrection. It would have occasioned only bewilderment. But something happened on that Sunday which explained why the tomb was found empty, and it sent the friends of Jesus into the streets with joy on their faces and courage in their hearts to proclaim that death had been unable to chain him.

This "something" was the appearance of Jesus, alive, to some of his friends, on the first Easter day. During the six weeks that followed there were many such meetings. The Gospels profess to give us only a selection of events in the story of Jesus (John 21:25), but even so there is an impressive catalog.

He appeared to Mary Magdalene (Mark 16:9; John 20:1-18), to the women (Matthew 28:1-10), to Simon Peter (Luke 24:34; 1 Corinthians 15:5), to the disciples on the road to Emmaus (Luke 24:13-31), to the eleven and other disciples (Matthew 28:16-20; Luke 24:36-49; John 20:19-23; 21:1-14; Acts 1:3-9; 1 Corinthians 15:5-6), to Thomas (John 20:24-29), to James (1 Corinthians 15:7), to Joseph and Matthias (Acts 1:22-23), to five hundred people at once (1 Corinthians 15:6), to Peter and John (John 21:15-24) and to Paul (Acts 9:4-6; 1 Corinthians 9:1; 15:8).

Together, these appearances to individuals and to groups, to men and to women, in country and in town, in the upper room and by the open lake, constitute testimony to the resurrection that has to be taken very seriously indeed.

Why, it might be asked, does Paul not refer in his catalog in 1 Corinthians 15 to the appearances of Jesus to the women? Answer: because he is summarizing the Jerusalem gospel tradition. And the Jerusalem gospel, proclaimed to Jews, would not have made use of testimony by women. One of the oldest commentaries on the Law of Moses states that evidence is not normally acceptable from a woman (Siphre on Deuteronomy, 190). In the light of this, is it not delightfully in character for Jesus to reveal himself alive first of all to despised women? And is it not totally incredible that if anybody had been fabricating the account of the resurrection they would have made its first witnesses women, people unqualified to give evidence?

The inclusion of Paul in the list is curious. The appearances ceased with the ascension of Jesus before the coming of the Spirit at Pentecost. It is as if Jesus spent six weeks showing them that he was indeed risen from the dead, training them for the world mission that awaited them, and then made a decisive break. From now on he would be known by the presence of his Spirit in their hearts, not by occasional appearances to a limited number of people. But Paul was persuaded that the Lord made an exception in his case.

Doubt it if you will. He did not doubt it. And he knew a vision when he saw one. As a matter of fact he regularly had visions, as he shows in 2 Corinthians 12:1-4, and he was clear that this was no vision. It left him physically blinded for a few days. Jesus was seen by him alone, but those with him heard the voice (Acts 9:7). He knew this appearance to him was an exception. The Lord "last of all, as to one untimely born, appeared also to me" (1 Corinthians 15:8), to commission this one-time opponent for the world mission which would make him Christ's most dedicated apostle. It is perhaps a reminder that however tidy your system, you can never predict what God will do.

Very well, there were these appearances. But what if they were hallucinations, seeming real enough to the people concerned, but devoid of objective reality?

The hallucination theory is at first sight attractive, but it is quite inadequate to explain the rise of the Christian movement, and it has serious weaknesses.

In the first place, only certain types of people are normally subject to hallucinations. Someone such as Mary Magdalene might fill the bill, but scarcely men with as diverse temperaments as Peter, Thomas, James and Paul!

Hallucinations are normally individual things. A man may believe he is a poached egg, but it is rare to find that many people from many different backgrounds all suffer from the same delusion. Here the same "hallucination" is observed by fishermen, tax-collectors, rabbis, close relations and five hundred people at once.

Hallucinations generally come to people who have been hankering after something for ages. The wish becomes father to the thought. But here we find no wish-fulfillment. As we have seen, the disciples were not expecting anything of the sort, and they were most reluctant to accept even the evidence of their own eyes.

Hallucinations tend to recur over a long period. Someone who suffers from them continues to suffer from them. But here they ceased as dramatically as they began. It all took place within six weeks.

Hallucinations are generally restricted to a particular person, a particular time and a particular place. In this case, the diversity could scarcely have been wider. The appearances took place at early morning, at noon, at night. Seashore, roadside, upper room, garden—the locality made no difference. And those who experienced these "seeings" were a very diverse bunch.

The appearances did not become increasingly bizarre, as is often the case with hallucinations. Rather, they remained very restrained in character—almost matter of fact. Moreover, far from mounting in frequency and pitch, as hallucinations often do, these meetings ceased entirely after forty days, never to recur.

The appearances seem to have an order and a logic

about them. They start in the garden by the tomb itself; they progress to Jerusalem and its environs; they move into Galilee on mountain and lake, and they direct the disciples to a mission into the whole world after their Lord is taken from them. These meetings, in fact, make plain Jesus' determination to leave them, assure them of his presence with them wherever they go, and prepare them for the worldwide commission. When the purpose of the resurrection appearances had been achieved, the need for them ceased. From now on the Jesus who had walked the streets of Palestine, the Jesus who had died and risen again, was with them by his Spirit in their hearts. That was the meaning of Pentecost. And Pentecost was the birthday of world mission.

3. The Christian Church

All over the world there exists a body called the church. It numbers somewhere in the region of 1,600 million people.

I am certainly not going to argue "so many can't be wrong." Numbers do not demonstrate truth.

But it is not without significance that Christianity traces its own origin to the resurrection of Jesus Christ. The church came into being around A.D. 30 because the first Christians were convinced that Jesus Christ was alive again. Had it not been for that, they would have scattered to their homes and forgotten all about their three years with Jesus. They would certainly not have founded a movement that withstood all the syncretism of ancient religion, triumphed over skepticism and persecution and became the one element in Roman civilization to survive the fall of Rome and spread into all the world.

It could be that these Christians were on to something! It could be that they were right in their radiant conviction that Jesus had risen from the dead, and that in his resurrection they had found the key to understanding the universe.

The rise of the church is undeniable. It is possible, of course, to maintain that they were wrong to trace their origins to the resurrection of Jesus, but that denial leaves us with some awkward questions to answer.

What else can account for the beginnings of the church? Let us suppose for a moment that Jesus did not rise, and that the disciples eventually recovered from the shock of his death enough to form a "Society of Jesus Veterans." They would have cherished old memories and talked (and written) of all he had done during those brief three years when they had known him. They would have said little publicly. That would have been to invite mockery. Their "guru" had, after all, ended up in failure and disgrace on a gibbet. And what would they have had to proclaim, anyhow? As for suggesting that others should cast in their lot with Jesus, that would have been unthinkable: he was dead and gone.

But, as we know, what happened was the very reverse of this. They did not gather to remember a dead Jesus but to celebrate a living one. In their letters they did not write about what he did in days gone by, but of what he, as Lord of the universe, was doing now. They did not even write their memoirs (or Gospels) until nearly a generation later when they were beginning to die off. Why not? They were too busy going round the world introducing people to the living Christ!

The growth and origin of the church is totally incredible if the resurrection is not true. Faith in the resurrection was what differentiated them from the Jewish establishment. But it was something they would not—they could not—give up. It happened to be true. It was the springboard for all their action.

What else can account for their success? The whole theme of their preaching was the resurrection, and it was proclaimed initially within a few minutes' walk of the tomb where Jesus had lain.

How can we explain the many thousands who became believers despite all that officialdom could do to stop them? How do we account for the fact that "a great many of the priests were obedient to the faith" (Acts 6:7)? How do we account for the fact that Saul, the great persecutor of the church, was converted and became the greatest champion of the resurrection faith he had labored so hard to destroy? How do we explain the fact that, unlike any other event in the past that loses its dynamism the further you are from it, this has not happened with the resurrection? More people would die for this belief today than at any other time in history.

I find it inconceivable that the church should have spread so fast and so widely had it been the case that the basic premise on which it was all founded, the resurrection, was false.

What else can explain their sacraments? As all the world knows, Christians have two ceremonies that are integral to their life and faith. One is baptism, the sacrament of Christian initiation. The other is the Holy Communion, the sacrament of Christian growth. Both are rooted in the resurrection.

Baptism was seen by the early Christians as re-enacting and personally appropriating the death and resurrection of Jesus: as the candidate goes into the water he dies to the old self-centered life and rises to a new life with Christ. "Do you not know that all of us who have been baptized into Christ Jesus were baptized into his death? We were buried therefore with him by baptism into death, so that as Christ was raised from the dead by the glory of the Father, we too might walk in newness of life" (Romans 6:3-4).

How could they have faced going through with a travesty like that if Jesus had not risen from the dead?

It was the same with "the Lord's Supper," as they called it. It was the Lord's not simply because it was held in memory of his sacrificial death on the cross, but because the Lord was present in their midst as they celebrated it. That is why we read that they broke bread with *agalliasis,* exultation (Acts 2:46). Unlike all the Greek community-feasts in honor of a dead hero, they rejoiced to share in communion with a living

Lord. You could not take part in the Lord's Supper without having the truth made very clear to you in the very action of the service.

What else can explain the change from Saturday to Sunday? Go to Israel today if you want to see how Jews guard their day of rest. It is a lesson to us all. They will not allow transport or any work on *shabbat,* the sabbath. It is sacred to the Lord. It is the day to commemorate his rest after creation. But these early Christians (all of them Jews, by the way) managed to change the very day of rest from Saturday to Sunday. Why? Because Sunday was the day Jesus rose from the dead, and they believed it was even more important to honor the day death died than the day life began.

It would be hard, very hard, to change the day off from Sunday to Monday these days. Yet we in the West have no such emotional and theological attachment to our day off as the Jews had, and have. Imagine how incredibly difficult it must have been to make such a change from the heart of Judaism. Yet that is what happened. It must have required some simply staggering happening to trigger such a thing.

The New Testament gives us one—the resurrection.

What else can explain the Christian conviction that Jesus is Lord? The earliest Christians, all of them Jews, were the most ardent of monotheists. Yet they acclaimed Jesus as divine. He was called "Lord," "My Lord and my God," "the Lamb who was slain and is in the midst of the throne," "the Son of God" and other such titles.

He was put on a par with God Almighty—and that *by Jews*, of all people! That simply blows the mind. How could they have been driven to the conviction that God Almighty had visited them in and through the person of Jesus? The answer must lie in the resurrection. He was "descended from David according to the flesh," so ran an ancient Christian creed, quoted by Paul in Romans 1:3-4, "and designated Son of God in power . . . by his resurrection from the dead."

That was it. That is why they served him as his "slaves," for so they delighted to call themselves. That is why they did not shrink from offering him worship.

Another ancient creed, springing from the days of the Aramaic-speaking church, puts it like this:

> Christ Jesus, who, though he was in the form of God, did not count equality with God a thing to be grasped, but emptied himself, taking the form of a servant, being born in the likeness of men. And being found in human form he humbled himself and became obedient unto death, even death on a cross. Therefore God has highly exalted him and bestowed on him the name which is above every name, that at the name of Jesus every knee should bow, in heaven and on earth and under the earth, and every tongue confess that Jesus Christ is Lord, to the glory of God the Father. (Philippians 2:6-11)

And just to rub it in, we must remember that every new Christian had to confess "Jesus is Lord" in his baptism. It is the earliest baptismal confession of the Christian church. And it is totally incomprehensible

67

without the resurrection.

The resurrection, of course, cannot be proved. No historical event can. All one can do is show that there is such a convergence of historical probabilities that the truth of the resurrection is placed beyond all reasonable doubt. In his book *The Resurrection of Christ*, A. M. Ramsey, later to become Archbishop of Canterbury, shows that "certain historical facts are unaccountable apart from the resurrection, and that different lines of historical testimony so converge as to point to the resurrection with overwhelming probability." It is, as Leslie Weatherhead puts it in *The Resurrection and the Life*, as if "half a dozen signposts, with the name of the same village painted on them, all point one way. Then sincerity in regard to the evidence compels belief that the village exists, even though we have never been there."

But the strongest evidence for the resurrection remains for the next chapter. It is afforded by those who *have* "been there."

MEETING
THE
MASTER
4

If the title of this chapter sounds a bit pious, you must forgive me. The fact of the matter is that personal encounter with Jesus Christ is the most powerful indicator that he rose from the dead.

The Power of Pentecost
Consider the earliest disciples. They took to the streets on the Day of Pentecost, seven weeks after the events of Holy Week. That delay alone would be very surprising had they been perpetrating a fraud. They were becoming acquainted with the risen Christ and then, obedient to his command, awaiting the coming of his Spirit into their lives.

At Pentecost he came. And the disciples thereupon caused a major disturbance in the temple courts. People thought they were drunk. But Peter, their spokesman, replied in effect, "That is nonsense. It is too early in the day to be drunk! But what God promised long ago has come true. He has given us his Spirit, the Spirit that lives in Jesus, whom you wickedly killed, but whom God has wonderfully raised from the dead. This is what accounts for the change you have noticed in us."

That was the thrust of Peter's speech that day. He and his friends were, as he describes it, "witnesses to the resurrection." Three thousand Jews were convinced by what he said and became Christians that very day.

These disciples had come alive in a big way. Gone were the crippling inhibitions that had kept them quiet in the previous seven weeks: they now preached ceaselessly. Gone was the cowardice that had kept them hidden away in the upper room: they were now as bold as brass for what they knew to be true. Neither prison, persecution, nor the threat of death could silence them. Many of them sealed their testimony with their blood.

Knowing the risen Christ to be in their midst, they even overcame their instinct for private ownership and shared their possessions with one another in a practical and loving communalism.

These were changed men, and all Jerusalem knew it.

It was just the same when the gospel spread to

pagan soil. In Athens the testimony of Christians caused a public debate (Acts 17). There was something new about them: the Athenians themselves put it down to "Jesus and the resurrection." At Philippi (Acts 16) their impact was so great that a riot ensued and they were put into prison. Result? They sang hymns at midnight, and the jailer and his family were converted! They made a big dent in the pagan licentiousness of Corinth, a city which was a byword for immorality. Many of the people who became Christians there had been involved in every kind of vice. But the power of the Spirit changed them. "Neither the immoral, nor idolaters, nor adulterers, nor sexual perverts, nor thieves, nor the greedy, nor drunkards, nor revilers, not robbers will inherit the kingdom of God," wrote Paul. "And such were some of you. But you were washed, you were sanctified, you were justified in the name of the Lord Jesus Christ and in the Spirit of our God" (1 Corinthians 6:9-11).

Such was the power of the living Christ. He could transform shameless pleasure-seekers, criminals, abandoned, self-centered people, and turn them into the church at Corinth. If the gospel could do that for the rakes at Corinth, then it spoke volumes for the truth of the resurrection.

It was to these same Corinthians that Paul wrote that fascinating piece about the resurrection we have already examined (1 Corinthians 15; see pp. 27-28). But we left one thing out. We did not look at the change of life which that short chronicle reveals. Paul tells them that "Christ died for our sins in accordance with the scriptures, that he was buried, that he was raised on the third day in accordance with the scriptures, and that he appeared to Cephas, then to the twelve. Then he appeared to more than five hundred brethren at one time, most of whom are still alive, though some have fallen asleep. Then he appeared to James, then to all the apostles. Last of all . . . he appeared also to me" (1 Corinthians 15:3-8).

The Testimony of Witnesses

What are these early witnesses saying? Not that they saw Jesus rise: it is one of the marks of the truthfulness of the New Testament that *nobody* claims that— whereas any fabricator could hardly have resisted producing eyewitnesses for such a *dénouement*. No, they make a more sober but in the end more far-reaching claim.

They bear witness to the fact that Jesus not only rose but *is alive*.

That comes out clearly in the tenses used in this remarkable ancient document. "Died," "was buried" and "appeared" are all in the aorist tense, the normal tense for past action. But the verb translated "he was raised to life" stands out like a sore thumb, for it is in the perfect tense. And the perfect is used when a past action has effects that remain until the present. So in that single word *egegertai* we see two crucial points. Not only did Jesus rise again from the dead on the third day, as a fact of history; he is still alive, and can be encountered. Such was the earliest Christian conviction about the resurrection, embedded in this document which derives from the thirties of the first century.

That is an absolutely staggering claim. What witnesses does Paul adduce to support it?

First "he appeared to Cephas (Peter)." That interview with the risen Jesus changed Peter from a vacillating, bombastic failure into the courageous leader we meet in the Acts, the man on whose testimony and example the early church was built.

Then the twelve come before us to give their testimony. They turned from a rabble who deserted their leader at his hour of trial into the church that was not afraid to face lions in the arena or execution from the government of their nation. For them, death was a defeated foe.

Thirdly, we are presented with James. He was the brother of Jesus (Mark 6:3), the child of Joseph and Mary, or maybe of Joseph by a former marriage. He was not a believer in Jesus during the days of his public ministry—far from it. Jesus' brothers did not believe in him: the whole family thought him deranged (John 7:5; Mark 3:21). But James too met with the risen Jesus. And he was dramatically changed by that encounter. He became the leader of the Jerusalem church.

Paul mentions that he appeared to "all the apostles." This would include Thomas, who was not with the disciples when Jesus first met them after his resurrection. But he was with them the second time. And he was invited to stretch out his finger and put it into the hole in Jesus' hands, and to stretch out his hand and thrust it into the spear-wound in his side. I don't suppose he needed to. He fell at the feet of Jesus, we are told, transformed by that resurrection encounter from skeptic to passionate follower. "My Lord and my God," he cried. He was a different man from that day onward. There is a strong tradition that he took the gospel to the south of India, where the ancient Mar Thoma Church exists to this day.

The "five hundred brethren at one time" are interesting. Some of them had died by the time Paul wrote to the Corinthians in A.D. 53. But most of them were still alive, he says. They must have been Galilean followers of Jesus who had known him during his ministry and had no doubt witnessed many of the events recorded in the Gospels. We hear no more about them. They are the forerunners of the hordes of nameless Christians who have been bearing witness to the risen Christ ever since. To such he is no dead historical figure, but a living contemporary, the supreme reality of their lives, with whom they share every experience and converse every day.

This is what Paul found Jesus to be. After years of service for the risen Master he could say artlessly "I know whom I have believed" (2 Timothy 1:12). He did not simply know about Jesus. He knew him. That original encounter changed his life and launched him into a relationship as intimate and daily renewed as marriage. His goal in life was simply this: to know

74

Jesus better (Philippians 3:10).

Any real Christian can say the same.

I can.

I well recall the day in my teens when I passed from *knowing about* Jesus to *knowing* him. I believed in a vague sort of way that he had risen, but it meant nothing to me. And then I was brought face to face with a number of teachers and fellow pupils in my school to whom it clearly meant a lot. I watched them. I observed the differences that this relation with Christ made in their lives. I wanted what they had. And one day I tentatively asked how I could find it. I came to see that if Jesus rose from the dead then he was alive—and I could meet him. Hesitantly, I put my life in his hands as best I knew how. And I have proved the reality of his presence ever since. It has gradually become the greatest certainty of my life.

Perhaps you think "It's all very well for you. You are a minister." True enough, but I should never have dreamed of becoming one had I not found that Jesus is alive.

However, I shall be glad to give you some twentieth-century witnesses who are not ministers.

The Life-Changing Power of the Resurrection

Michelle is a white South African graduate, a highly intelligent mathematician. She was born into a Jewish family, but in the course of her studies at Cape Town University had been impressed by the Christians she knew. She came to encounter the living Christ for herself, and that meeting changed her life. She wrote at the time of her baptism, "I think this is one of the most wonderful facets of Christianity, the great joy it brings. When I was telling someone else about it over the phone, they said they could *hear* how happy I sounded. . . . Before my baptism I was scared to admit to my Jewish friends that I was a Christian, but now I want the whole world to know." And now guess where she is? She is married to a Christian and working with him as a missionary in Kenya. Quite a change for a white South African!

I think of a group of unemployed boys in Lima, Peru. Unemployed, that is, until the Christians began to set up a small leather-work shop for them to learn a trade in. They got a new leather-work teacher. And their first question? "Is he a brother?" He was not, in the sense they meant it. So they set about introducing him to the living Christ. Friendship with Jesus was the paramount concern of their lives.

I think of an Ethiopian who has come to Oxford to study and has found the risen Christ. He is thrilled with the Lord and enthusiastic in speaking about him to his fellow overseas students.

A Polish girl who lives in Warsaw comes from a militantly atheistic home. She was invited to a meeting of Christian young people and was fascinated by their evident joy as they spoke of Jesus. Soon afterward she happened to sit next to a Christian on a bus. He spoke simply to her about the risen Christ and secretly she believed. She found in her own heart the reality of which the others had spoken, and after a week she mustered the courage to tell her parents. They were furious. She was kicked out of home. But it did not rob her of her peace of mind and her infectious joy. The result? Her parents are now asking questions. They want what she has.

This is how a university teacher in computer science has described to me her appreciation of the encounter with Christ that has changed her life:

The best thing that has ever happened to me was the dawning awareness that Jesus Christ was not just a historic figure; a good man dead and gone. Mysterious though it seems, he is the Son of God who died on behalf of all, rose from the dead and now offers life to any who dare to trust him. I have taken this step of faith. I know I am alive. Jesus has brought strong and consistent meaning to my life. More than anything in the world I want to live my life for him. I want him to be my Number One. Walking with Jesus through life is the most liberating of all possible relationships. Jesus understands me better than I can ever hope to understand myself. Gradually, he is releasing me from my "hang-ups" and enabling me to discover and to become the person he wants me to be. His capacity for loving and forgiving is endless. He forgives me even when I cannot forgive myself. Nothing can ever separate him from me, so I am never alone.

If Jesus were not alive I could not be writing as I am. His love for me brings a security and hope in this unstable and changing world. Living for him, motivated and helped by his Spirit within, is the biggest challenge anyone could be given. Perhaps the words of Dom Julian best express what I feel most deeply:

If everything is lost, thanks be to God.
If I must see it go, watch it go,
Watch it fade away, die,
Thanks be to God that he is all I have
And if I have him not, I have nothing at all.

This is the sort of testimony that many of our contemporaries bear to Jesus Christ. They speak of what they actually know of him from their own experience.

That may not seem very satisfactory. It might be tidier if it were possible to prove the matter one way or the other. But life is not like that. It simply is not possible to put into words an experience that has changed your life, let alone prove it. That is what a Ghanian friend of mine was struggling to say when he wrote: "I know Jesus lives, because I meet him every day, and share fellowship with him. Fellowship can only exist between people who are *living*. I think that the truth that Jesus lives is something that one can experience rather than describe."

That is true enough. And it is borne out by this story a Czechoslovakian theologian told me. A Russian lecturer, a member of the Communist party, was addressing a packed audience on the subject of the resurrection of Jesus Christ. He spoke at considerable length, seeking to discredit it. At the end, an Orthodox

priest rose and asked if he might reply. He was warned that he could only have five minutes. "Five seconds is all I shall need" was his reply. He turned to the audience, and gave the delightful Easter greeting, characteristic of the Eastern church. *"Christos aneste,"* he cried, "Christ is risen." Back with a deafening roar came the traditional reply from the crowded hall, *"Alethos aneste,"* "Truly he is risen."

That is the essence of the Christian witness through the centuries. It has not changed since some of the disciples encountered Jesus on the first Easter day.

The heart of the matter for the Christian is this: Jesus did not merely rise, he is alive, alive and ready to be met by men, women or children who are willing to share their lives with him.

That is not the common image of Christianity. God forgive us, we have smothered the risen Christ in denominationalism, ecclesiasticism, respectability, moralism, and goodness knows what else. But that is the heart of authentic Christianity.

Christians are the "community of the resurrection." They are like iron filings attracted by and adhering to the magnetic person of Jesus Christ, risen from the dead.

It is impossible to do justice to the evidence for the resurrection unless you take into account this worldwide testimony from believers great and small that Jesus is not a dead hero but a living Lord. The changes he can make to life at all levels will be the subject of our next chapter.

DRAWING
THE
IMPLICATIONS
5

The resurrection of Jesus was never intended to be a matter for academic discussion. It has the most practical of implications and ought never to be considered apart from them.

When Paul discusses the resurrection in 1 Corinthians 15, he shows a ruthless integrity in drawing the implications. If Jesus did not rise from the grave, then Paul's preaching has been a waste of time, their faith is futile and they remain unforgiven. What is more, all Christians misrepresent God, dead Christians are finished and live Christians are deluded! That is how he summarizes the situation in verses 12-19 of that chapter.

On the other hand, if Christ did rise, he is alive to be encountered (verses 4-8), he has cleared our accusing past (verse 3), he has broken the fear of death (verse 54), his resurrection is the pledge of our own (verse 22), he can change human nature (verse 57) and he has a plan for our lives (verse 58). In other words, it is impossible to exaggerate the importance, for practical everyday concerns, of the resurrection of Jesus from the dead.

Let us take a look at some of the implications of the resurrection.

Death Is Not the End

For centuries men and women have been wrestling with the question: is death the end? Are we snuffed out like a candle, or is death the doorway to some future life? There are plenty of arguments, plenty of speculations, plenty of séances. But there would be only one certain way to find out—that is if someone had died and had come back, not just to die again in due course, but as the undisputed conqueror of death.

Jesus Christ has achieved just that. He has returned from the grave and has demonstrated that there is indeed a life after death. If we insist on reckoning without that factor of life after death we are being foolishly shortsighted. For by his resurrection Jesus has "forced open a door that had been locked since the death of the first man. He has met, fought, and beaten the king of death. Everything is different because he has done so. This is the beginning of the new

creation: a new chapter in cosmic history has opened."
So wrote C. S. Lewis in *Miracles*.

Such is the sober truth, ever since the day death
died. For, enigmatic though it seems, that is precisely
what happened. Death has had its fangs drawn, its
finality reversed.

No longer need men face death as Dylan Thomas
advised:

> Do not go gentle into that good night,
> Old age should burn and rave at close of day;
> Rage, rage against the dying of the light.

In days gone by there was nothing to look for but

> the dread of something after death,
> the undiscovered country from whose bourne
> no traveler returns.

But now a traveler has returned. It is no longer an
undiscovered country. Easter spelled the day when
death, in all its fearsome finality, died, and a way was
opened up to that country of eternal life for which so
many had longed, but of whose existence there was
no clear proof.

The Religion to Follow

Ours is a day of syncretism. All religions are common-
ly thought to be much the same. It is not supposed to
matter which you choose. But Christianity refuses to

be sucked into this indifferentism. It has always refused.

Is this because Christians are uncharitable and narrowminded? Not at all. It is simply that Jesus Christ claimed to be the way to God, the truth about God and the very life of God. He vindicated that claim by the resurrection. Jesus said, "All things have been delivered to me by my Father; and no one knows the Son except the Father, and no one knows the Father except the Son and any one to whom the Son chooses to reveal him" (Matthew 11:27). A staggering claim, but one that he made good by the resurrection.

The resurrection, therefore, is the place to begin if you are looking for a satisfying faith on which to base your life. Do not waste a lot of time investigating every religion under the sun from animism to Hinduism. Examine the evidence for the resurrection of Jesus Christ instead. If he is risen you need look no further.

You will, of course, find much to admire, much to learn from, in other religions (as well as a lot of filth and cruelty): the God of the whole earth has not left himself without witness. But you will not find in them anything good and true that cannot be found in Christ. And nowhere else will you find out about a God who cares enough for you to die for you, to rise from the grave as a pledge of your future, and to be willing to come and share his life with you.

If Jesus is, as the resurrection asserts, God himself come to our rescue, then to reject him, or even to ignore him, is ultimate folly. That is why Jesus is not, and never can be, just one among the many religious leaders of mankind. He is not even the best. He is the only. Among many examples of the relative he stands out as the absolute. In the risen Jesus, God Almighty confronts us with shattering directness. He offers us total succor, but he asks of us total allegiance.

It is sensible to have an interest in comparative religion. But the more you know of the others, the more clearly Christianity is seen to be unique. And the heart of Christianity is the resurrection.

The point is well made by the famous meeting of Auguste Comte, the French philosopher, and Thomas Carlyle. Comte said he intended to found a new religion that would sweep away Christianity and everything else in its wake. He was very enthusiastic about it. Carlyle's devastating reply ran something like this: "Splendid. All you need to do is to speak as never man spoke, to live as never man lived, to be crucified, rise again the third day, and get the world to believe you are still alive. Then your religion will have some chance of success."

Jesus, the Son of God
Jesus made many remarkable claims during his lifetime. He claimed the right to forgive sins (Mark 2:10) and to accept worship (Luke 5:8); he claimed he would separate sheep and goats at the last judgment (Matthew 25:31ff.); he claimed to be the light of the world, the bread of life and the resurrection (John 8:12; 6:48; 11:25).

Many people did not believe him. So he made his credibility hang on the resurrection. Refusing their request for a compulsive sign, Jesus said, "An evil and adulterous generation seeks for a sign; but no sign shall be given to it except the sign of the prophet Jonah. For as Jonah was three days and three nights in the belly of the whale, so will the Son of man be three days and three nights in the heart of the earth" (Matthew 12:39-40).

And from the earliest days after the resurrection, his followers began to realize the staggering implications. He fulfilled all the hopes of the Old Testament scriptures! So he *was* the prophet like Moses, he *was* the Son of man of whom Daniel had prophesied, he *was* the Suffering Servant of Isaiah, he *was* the Messiah, so long awaited by the Jews. All this and more. He was no less than God's "Son"—distinct from the heavenly Father, and yet one with him. Peter proclaimed this as early as the Day of Pentecost. Paul cited the early creed we have already looked at in Romans 1:3-4: he was "descended from David according to the flesh and designated Son of God in power . . . by his resurrection." Paul wrote, "In him the whole fulness of deity dwells bodily" (Colossians 2:9).

So Jesus was not just a great teacher and a splendid man. He was no latter-day Confucius, no Jewish edition of Socrates. He was shown by the resurrection to be no less than he claimed to be, the Savior, the Messiah, the Son of man, the Son of God, the way to God. Because Christ rose to a new and eternal life, he can

86

no longer be classified among men of excellence. He was indeed completely human: but he is nothing less than God. And as God he claims our worship and our allegiance.

The Atonement for Our Sins

The New Testament is insistent that "all have sinned and fall short of the glory of God," that "none is righteous, no, not one" (Romans 3:10, 23), and that all the world is guilty before God. That is unpalatable, but we know it is true.

We also know that even if we could live a perfect life from now on, this could do nothing to wipe out the past. Reluctantly we assent to the humbling verdict of the Bible: "No man can deliver his own soul."

But as Jesus told us, he came "to give his life as a ransom for many" (Matthew 20:28). And on the cross he did just that. The darkness at Calvary gives us an insight into the darkness that stifled his soul when "the Lord laid on him the iniquity of us all," as the prophet Isaiah had put it centuries before.

Peter, who was perhaps an eyewitness at the edge of the crowd, picked up that theme of Isaiah's and declared, "He himself bore our sins in his body on the tree," and again, "Christ also died for sins once for all, the righteous for the unrighteous, that he might bring us to God" (1 Peter 2:24; 3:18).

All the New Testament writers agree. This is what the cross means: God has not abandoned us—rather, he has himself undertaken the enormous ransom, the vast debt incurred by human sinfulness. Well might John write "God is love . . . not that we loved God but that he loved us and sent his Son to be the expiation for our sins" (1 John 4:8, 10).

But was his sacrifice enough? Was even the death of the Son of God sufficient cover, so to speak, for all our liabilities? Could God Almighty, as the hymn puts it, justly "look on him and pardon me"?

There would have been no way of answering that question had not Jesus risen from the dead. We could not have been sure whether his death-cry, "It is finished" (John 19:30), was a cry of defeat or a shout of victory. But the resurrection made it crystal clear. The resurrection was God's "Yes" to the achievement of Calvary. It was God's vindication of his precious Son. It was the demonstration that he could, because of what Jesus did on Calvary, forgive (indeed, acquit) any who came to him trusting in what Jesus had done. He was "put to death for our trespasses and raised for our justification." Such is the triumphal conclusion of Romans 4:25.

Down through the ages the cross and resurrection have spelled peace for troubled consciences. I shall never forget the joy on the face of one student when he understood it. He had in fact made a list of the things burdening his conscience and had brought it along with him. But as he came to understand what Jesus through his cross and resurrection had done to his failures, there was only one thing to do with that list: we tore it into little pieces!

Bunyan put it picturesquely in *Pilgrim's Progress:*
As Christian came up with the cross his burden
loosed from off his shoulders and fell from his back.
It began to tumble, and continued to do so till it
came to the mouth of the sepulchre where it fell
in, and I saw it no more.

Then was Christian glad and lightsome, and said
with a merry heart, "He hath given me rest by his
sorrow, and life by his death." . . . Then Christian
gave three leaps for joy, and went on singing.

That is how it appeared to John Bunyan three hundred years ago in Bedford prison. This is how it appears to Michael Alison, a British politician:

My conviction about the certainty of the resurrection is based upon the profound sense of forgiveness which I enjoy, in dissociating myself from the dark deeds I have done or might do, and associating them with the dead and mutilated Christ. My "old self" is, in a way I can actually experience with inward conviction, done away with and destroyed in Christ. The profoundest element in my fellowship with God lies precisely in this: that he can allow himself to be destroyed by the worst in me, and yet can come back loving! Without the actual fellowship of loving God in Christ, the past transference of guilt would be a mere expediency, a cause for deepening, not relieving, self-centeredness and remorse.

A Continual Companion

The final promise of Jesus Christ, recorded in the

last verse of Matthew's Gospel, is this: "Lo, I am with you always, to the close of the age."

His followers are promised no picnic, no safe passage. But they are told that whatever befalls them cannot rob them of his presence.

Paul was acutely aware of this. As he lay in prison he was able to write "Rejoice in the Lord always; again I will say, Rejoice. . . . The Lord is at hand" (Philippians 4:4-5). And when he was reflecting on the enormous forces of opposition that he and his mission for Christ had stirred up, he took comfort from this fact, that the living Lord was with him, and would be to the end. "Who shall separate us from the love of Christ? Shall tribulation, or distress, or persecution, or famine, or nakedness, or peril, or sword?" (Romans 8:35). Christ offers us his constant presence, and no other security.

But that offer is enough. For loneliness is a killer. You can be more lonely in a crowd than on a desert island. Loneliness is one of the main causes of suicide among students, of despair among the old. It is not surprising that the famous painter Annigoni, when asked what picture he would most like to be remembered by, replied "Solitude." He was so impressed by the loneliness of modern man that he has painted no less than twelve studies of it.

Jesus promised to meet this gnawing need by his presence in the hearts and lives of his followers: he even offered to become our friend. "I have called you friends," he says (John 15:15), and that friendship is beyond value. Charles Kingsley was once asked the most significant thing in his experience, and he replied enigmatically, "I had a Friend."

Somebody expressed it to me a little more explicitly: "Jesus is the only person with whom I can communicate in every situation, knowing immediately that he has understood completely. . . . I find it difficult to believe that he loves me and cares about the smallest as well as the largest details of my life; that he is willing and able to forgive me time after time for doing what I know to be wrong. But experience has shown that all this is true and I am assured it always will be."

That friendship with Christ is what enables the Christian to be somewhat independent of the approval or disapproval of the crowd. He is not squeezed into the conventional mold by the pressures of public opinion or social custom. He has a friend, and in that friendship lies his security. So "keep your life free from love of money, and be content with what you have; for he has said 'I will never fail you nor forsake you.' Hence we can confidently say, 'The Lord is my helper, I will not be afraid; what can man do to me?' " (Hebrews 13:5-6).

Moral Power

Our trouble is not only our guilt and loneliness, but our inability to do what is right. Like the apostle Paul, we have so often to admit "I can will what is right, but I cannot do it. For I do not do the good I want, but

91

the evil I do not want is what I do" (Romans 7:18-19). There is a moral weakness in every one of us, and try as we may, we cannot eradicate it.

But this is where the power of the risen Christ comes in. He lived a perfect life, and if he comes to share life with us, we can surely turn to him in moments of temptation and ask for his strength to take over and replace our weakness. "I can do all things," wrote Paul, "in him who strengthens me" (Philippians 4:13).

There is a most illuminating prayer of his, recorded in his letter to Christians at Ephesus (1:19-20a). He prays that they may know "what is the immeasurable greatness of his power in us who believe, according to the working of his great might which he accomplished in Christ when he raised him from the dead." In other words, the very power exerted by God in raising Christ from the dead is available to raise us from the failures to which we are so prone by nature.

History is full of examples that show the truth of this wonderful promise. Men like Augustine and John Newton, deeply sunk in vice, became models of Christian living once they surrendered to the power of the living Christ.

In my own experience as a Christian, I have seen him transform the lives of prostitutes, drug addicts, swindlers, and people caught in the toils of the occult. I have seen compulsive gamblers and alcoholics changed. His touch still heals.

There is nothing automatic about it. He does not give us power if we do not want it and ask for it—and often we don't. Moreover, we do not become Christ-like all at once. It is a gradual process of transformation.

Nevertheless, the power of the living Jesus is able to handle any specific temptation that we hand over to him, and to give us power to overcome it. In this way we become "more than conquerors through him who loved us" (Romans 8:37). Conquerors—yes. But *more than* conquerors, because through the conflict and the temptation we learn to trust him more and get to know him better. So let none of us think our temptations are too great to bear. They are not too great for him to bear. "No temptation has overtaken you that is not common to man. God is faithful, and he will not let you be tempted beyond your strength, but with the temptation will also provide the way of escape, that you may be able to endure it" (1 Corinthians 10:13). The "way of escape" is to ask him for his strength, early on in the process of temptation, *and really to want it!*

Resurrection Joy
It brought joy to the first disciples when Jesus rose and made himself known to them. He told them that joy would be his parting gift to them, and so it has proved. The pages of Christian history re-echo with joy and laughter, for he does not come alongside us in order to rob us or make us miserable, but to give us life at its very best. "I came that they may have life, and have it abundantly" he said (John 10:10b). And

that is in striking contrast to the disenchantment and dissatisfaction that are such notable features of our day.

There is normally a tremendous sense of joy when a person turns his life over to Jesus Christ. Of course: the long resistance is over, and the creature is reconciled with his Creator. But that initial excitement does not last, any more than it does in marriage. It gives way to something less bubbly and more profound: a deep sense of contentment.

A bedridden man suffering from an incurable disease wrote of this inner contentment: "Christ has made it possible for me to accept suffering without inner resentment, bitterness or boredom. Those are the burdens he has taken from me. He has given me in return peace of heart, joy and illumination during the lonely hours, and a focus of attention always away from myself, because there is so much work to be done for him even when I am flat on my back."

I have noticed this joy most, I think, among Christians who have few of the things we normally prize—money, security, a nice home. I have noticed it among the poor in third-world countries. I have noticed it among Christians in the face of death.

I think of a dear friend, Archbishop Janani Luwum of Uganda, who was martyred by President Idi Amin. Janani had to tell Amin that the church could not go along with his murders and injustice: the President was furious and determined to do away with Janani. But the Archbishop did not flinch, and he did not quit. He knew what was coming to him, and when, like his Master, he was arraigned and falsely accused, he said nothing, only gently shook his head in denial of the charges. When taken downstairs to the torture chamber, he found another believer, and together they fell on their knees to pray to God for their persecutor. That is what I mean by joy. There was a calm sense that all was in the hands of a loving God, and that nothing could separate them from the companionship of a living Christ. That is a joy worth having.

A Community with a Purpose

There is something very fragmentary about Western society. We think and act individualistically. God never intended us to live that way, but rather as a community in dependence upon him.

The resurrection makes that possible.

It is noteworthy that in the Gospels the disciples were rescued from their loneliness and despair by the resurrection. Each one did not go off and do his own thing: we find them being together, praying and eating together, witnessing together on the street and in the synagogues. It is to the disciples *as a community* that Jesus gave his commission to go and spread the gospel throughout the world, according to both Matthew and John. It is to the disciples *as a community* that the Spirit came.

In a society that is falling apart, this aspect of the resurrection cannot be stressed too strongly. Once we get in touch with the living Christ he puts us deeply in touch with others in his church. Linked to the head, we inevitably take our place among other limbs in the body and find the thrill of being caught up in Christ's mission.

I think of a small-time gardener in a Latin American country. Illiterate and ignorant, he could well be spending a very narrow life. But far from it. He is the lay pastor of a tiny church, some twenty strong, which meets in his house. All the members tell of what Christ is doing in their lives, and they are growing in love and usefulness. The risen Christ has not only come into this man's individual life: he has made him into what he was intended to be and put him in touch both with his God and his fellow believers.

I think of a sophisticated university lecturer who, when first I knew him, was arrogant and critical. But now it is all very different. He has come to a deep trust in the living Christ, and the results in his life have been remarkable. Gone is that old critical attitude. Gone is the proud isolation. He is very much part of the extraordinarily mixed local church community to which he belongs, and one of the parish house groups meets in his home. He sees himself as part of a community that is, for all its failings, a first installment of God's kingdom, a community marked by the resurrection.

The Pledge of Our Resurrection
Jesus assured his disciples that he was going away at his death, to prepare for them a place in the Father's

house. Had this not been the case, he would have told them (John 14:2).

That was quite a claim. But it became credible after the resurrection of Jesus.

If he had risen to a new quality of life beyond the grave, there was good reason to suppose that he could bring his followers there too. Paul, therefore, can say, "But in fact Christ has been raised from the dead, the first fruits of those who have fallen asleep" (1 Corinthians 15:20). Where there are first fruits, there is also a crop to come. That is why the book of Revelation can exclaim, "Blessed are the dead who die in the Lord" (Revelation 14:13). Death for the Christian is not, as society supposes, the worst thing that can befall you. It takes you out of one room in the Father's house, the room of faith, into another room, the room of sight. You will be with the Lord.

An old Christian man lay dying, and he asked his doctor, also a Christian, if he had any convictions about what lay before him after death. The doctor fumbled for an answer. Then there was heard a scratching at the door. "Do you hear that?" he asked his patient. "That is my dog. I left him downstairs, but he grew impatient and has come up here, and can hear my voice. He has no idea of what lies beyond this door, but he knows that I am here. Now is it not like that with you? You do not know what lies beyond the door, but you know your Master is there."

What that life will be like we cannot say in any detail, nor need we try. Two hints are contained in 1 Corinthians 15. The first indicates that we shall be like Jesus. "Just as we have borne the image of the man of dust, we shall also bear the image of the man of heaven" (15:49). The second indicates that the splendor of that life after death will be analogous to the whole ear of wheat compared to the shriveled grain which was put into the ground (15:35-38). If you had never seen a plant of wheat growing, you would be amazed to discover that it came from that little seed of dry grain you had planted the previous autumn, wouldn't you? Right, says Paul, it is like that with the resurrection. As with the wheat seed, there will be a continuity of life going right through the process of death. As with the wheat seed, the final state will be far more wonderful than the first. It will in fact be like the resurrection body of Jesus—identifiable, but no longer subject to the limitations of time and space and decay. And that is something to look forward to.

Christianity does not teach the immortality of the soul, but the resurrection of the body. There is no question of the flight of the alone to the Alone, or absorption into the archetypal One. It is rather a matter of personal and undying relationships between redeemed persons and their Lord. Nor is there a question of crass materialism, as if the very stuff of this present body were essential to our future state: "God gives it a body as he has chosen. . . . There are heavenly bodies and there are earthly bodies; but the glory of the heavenly is one, and the glory of the earthly is another" (1 Corinthians 15:38, 40).

There is a lovely passage in which Martin Luther wrestles with the problem of life after death, and revels in the confidence that Christ's resurrection affords:

Just as one does not know how it happens that one falls asleep and suddenly morning approaches when one awakes, so we will suddenly be resurrected at the last day, not knowing how we have come into death and through death. We shall sleep until he comes and knocks at the tomb and says "Dr. Martin, get up!" Then in one moment I will get up and will rejoice with him in eternity.

A New Attitude to Death

Don't believe people if they tell you that they do not fear death. The fear of death holds modern civilization in a vicelike grip, and it is nonetheless real for being driven underground. William Butler Yeats caught this shrewdly in his poem *Death*.

Nor dread nor hope attend
A dying animal;
A man awaits his end
Dreading and hoping all.

But the wonderful thing about the resurrection of Jesus is that it gives a solid ground for hope. Here is one who has died, risen and assures believers they will be with him in the afterlife. What is there to fear?

Paul put his finger on the really awesome thing about death: it finalizes our state of sinful rebellion against God, our constant breaking of his law. If he is just, then this is something he cannot overlook. But

99

if Christ has borne our condemnation, then the fangs of death have been drawn. "Death is swallowed up in victory. O death, where is thy victory? O death, where is thy sting?" Paul is quoting the Old Testament. He then continues on his own account, "The sting of death is sin, and the power of sin is the law. But thanks be to God, who gives us the victory through our Lord Jesus Christ" (1 Corinthians 15:54-56).

The writer to the Hebrews eloquently makes the same point when he says that one of the main reasons Jesus came to share our flesh and blood was "that through death he might destroy him who has the power of death, that is, the devil, and deliver all those who through fear of death were subject to lifelong bondage" (Hebrews 2:14-15).

The living Christ really does remove the fear of death.

I have just been reading the story of the first converts in Uganda a hundred years ago. Several were pages at the court of the Kabaka of Buganda, and they were arrested and burned alive. They refused to deny Christ. Instead they burst into song—the hymn "Daily, daily, sing the praises of the city God has made"— while the youngest, little Yusufu (only eleven years of age) said, "Please do not cut off my arms. I will not struggle in the fire that takes me to Jesus."

But it is not only our fear of death that the resurrection of Jesus can transform, but also our attitude to bereavement.

When a Christian loved one dies we need not be

left desolate. We have three precious gifts. First, the promise of the risen Lord: "Where I am there you shall be also." That departed one is with the Lord and is better off than we are. Then we have the people of the risen Lord: he has given us brethren to "rejoice with those that rejoice and weep with those that weep." The Christian family can make an enormous and lasting difference to enduring and overcoming bereavement. And finally, we have the promise of the risen Lord: "I am with you always." We shall sorrow, to be sure, but not as those who have no hope. We shall weep, but not inconsolably. There will be a great reunion one day, and the pledge of that is the living Lord who holds both us and the dead believer in his grip, a grip even death cannot break (1 Thessalonians 4:16-18).

I shall not soon forget a couple whose only daughter had been killed by a careless motorist shortly after coming to Oxford to train as an occupational physiotherapist. My friends were full of grief, but also full of hope—the living Lord was very real to them. We had a luncheon in my house for the funeral party after the service, and the father spoke to the assembled guests and told what Christ meant to him. They were amazed—so was an agnostic girl who had come to see me, arrived early, and had been brought into the lunch-party. Somehow her list of objections to the Christian faith (which she had prepared to test me with) faded into irrelevance. She had seen something of what Christ can do in bereavement, and it was one of the factors that brought her to faith soon afterwards.

A Pointer to the Future of the World

There is a lot in the Bible about God preparing a new heaven and a new earth, with new people to live in them. It is beautiful and poetic, and we might be inclined to leave it at that, were it not for the resurrection. But in this one person, the new creation has already taken place.

Perhaps God still has a purpose for this world of ours. Perhaps he will take the constituent elements within it and recreate them for something new. In any event, the resurrection of the body of Jesus seems to be a sign that God is interested in reordering rather than scrapping this universe he has made with such care.

Dr. Roger Pilkington, in his book *World Without End,* has offered this interpretation of the resurrection of Jesus. It is worth pondering. "If matter is no more than an arrangement of energy, then it is perfectly conceivable (if surprising) that where the sheer essence of the whole creation was poured into human form, the body could dissociate into sheer energy and redistill, as it were, outside the tomb, in a state which was, on the average, more energy than matter, but definitely material enough to have some shape and substance."

Could it be that what took place in Christ at the mid-point of history is a pointer to God's purpose for the new creation, of which Christ is the head, at the end? One day we shall know!

I was very struck recently in seeing how a brilliant philosopher, literary man, and man of action, Jean-Paul Sartre, faced the future of mankind. He was a passionate atheist who in earlier life had written books such as *Nausea* and had not flinched from drawing the most fearless consequences from atheism. In 1980 he wrote in a journal on the subject of despair and hope:

> With this third world war which might break out one day, with this wretched gathering which our planet now is, despair returns to tempt me. The idea that there is no purpose, only petty personal ends for which we fight! We make little revolutions, but there is no goal for mankind. One cannot think such things. They tempt you incessantly, especially if you are old and think "Oh well, I'll be dead in five years at the most." In fact, I think ten, but it might well be five. In any case the world seems ugly, bad, and without hope. There, that's the cry of despair of an old man who will die in despair. But that's exactly what I resist. I know I shall die in hope. But that hope needs a foundation.

It does indeed.

That foundation is the empty grave and living presence of Jesus Christ. You will find it nowhere else.

Alas, within a month Sartre was dead: did he find that foundation which he longed for?

The Resurrection in Our Lives

Before we leave the implications of the resurrection, there is one very important one that Christians tend to ignore. It is that the cross and resurrection of Jesus are intended to find a counterpart in our lives. "He himself bore our sins in his body on the tree, that we might die to sin and live to righteousness," or "We were buried . . . with him by baptism into death, so that as Christ was raised from the dead by the glory of the Father, we too might walk in newness of life," or "always carrying in the body the death of Jesus, so that the life of Jesus may also be manifested in our bodies" (1 Peter 2:24, Romans 6:4, 2 Corinthians 4:10).

The point is this. The cross and resurrection are not merely external to us. They must become part of us. There needs to be a real dying to sin and self-centeredness in each one of us. And there needs to be a real appropriating of the power and radiance of the resurrection. You cannot have the power of the resurrection without being willing to tread the way of the cross. You cannot have the crown without the thorns. Triumphalism, therefore, has no place in authentic Christianity. There will be triumph, but it will be the triumph of the crucified. The Corinthians wanted the power of the resurrection without going the way of the cross. Paul told them it could not be done: that is why he was determined to "know nothing among you except Jesus Christ and him crucified" (1 Corinthians 2:2).

Part of the paradox, part of the "in-between-ness"

of being a Christian in this age, is that we are both subject to the pain and fallenness of a world that has run amok *and* are also heirs of the kingdom of God with all its power and glory. Many Christians are unaware of the power that God means them to have, the very power of the resurrection itself. Many Christians who do know that power have forgotten that they cannot escape the self-sacrifice and suffering. As ever, Paul had the balance. His aim was "that I may know him and the power of his resurrection, and may share his sufferings, becoming like him in his death, that if possible I may attain the resurrection from the dead" (Philippians 3:10-11).

Those are just some of the implications of the greatest event in history, the resurrection of Jesus Christ from the dead.

TAKING THE PLUNGE

6

Of all the remarkable sermons in the Acts of the Apostles, none is more astonishing than Paul's address at Athens. It is recorded in Acts 17.

We are confronted with the most sophisticated city in the ancient world: cultured, civilized Athens. And in the foreground skeptical, cynical *dilettanti* who "spent their time in nothing except telling or hearing something new" (verse 21). They belonged to contrasting outlooks on life. The Epicureans were pleasure-seekers; the Stoics put duty first. And Paul takes them all on. Paul the traveler, the theologian, but above all the evangelist, whose "spirit was provoked within him as he saw that the city was full of idols" (Acts 17:16).

Paul in Athens

What did he have to say to this formidable audience, when they gave him a full hearing? It wasn't a fashionable message. Oh, to be sure he began where they were, using the local landscape for a text. As he passed through the city he noticed an inscription "to an unknown God." The traveler Pausanias, a century later, records altars of Athens to "gods both named and unknown." So Paul set out to introduce them to the "unknown God" whom they worshiped but did not know. He was the God who had made heaven and earth, and had created all people with the express purpose that they should seek after him and find him. Mankind has refused to turn to the Creator and has replaced him with various idols. Nevertheless God has overlooked all that—until Christ came.

> But now he commands all men everywhere to repent, because he has fixed a day on which he will judge the world in righteousness by a man whom he has appointed, and of this he has given assurance to all men by raising him from the dead. (Acts 17:30-31)

Could anything be more inappropriate than a message like that before so civilized an audience? All this talk of repentance, judgment and resurrection? Yet that is what Paul did. And he was right. Paul knew the dangers of endless intellectual discussion, of playing with serious issues. So he gives this strong, peremptory challenge. We need to heed it just as much as they did in first-century Athens.

Take a close look at that remarkable challenge.

Whom does God command to repent? All people. No less. Pleasure seekers must repent. Conscientious hard-working Stoics must repent—for they too have sinned and fallen short of the standards of a holy God. He offers forgiveness on the grounds of what Jesus did on the cross. But nobody can have that forgiveness until he repents.

Repentance is not a matter of beating the breast and pretending to be very wicked and very contrite. It is a matter of letting go all you know to be wrong and coming to the Lord to ask him to forgive you, accept you, and turn you in a new direction. It is absolutely indispensable. Nobody has ever become a member of God's family without it. That is why God does not suggest it or advise it. He commands it. And if it is *God* who commands all men to repent, only a fool would ignore it.

God might very well have left it there, but he did not. He cares too much. So he gave a reason for his command.

Why should we repent? Because he has fixed the day when he will judge mankind, and judge them by the standard of Jesus Christ. That is why it is so important to repent and get right with him.

Can you face the judgment of God with confidence?

I can't. My words and actions, my thoughts and attitudes, the wrong things I've done and the good things I haven't done, all crowd in on me. "My sins have taken such hold upon me that I am not able to look up," said the psalmist. I feel a bit like that—not at all confident at facing the perfect justice of a holy God.

And it will be absolutely fair. I will be judged—you will be judged—by no alien standard, but by what it means to be fully alive, fully human. The standard will be man as he ought to be, Jesus. His love will show up our apathy, his unselfishness our greed, his purity our lust, his integrity our deceit. We shall be compared with him.

Need I say what the verdict will be?

That accounts for the urgency of Paul's plea. The gospel is not something to be debated, but to be acted upon. We need to repent because if we do not there is no hope for us. We shall be judged. And we shall be condemned. Not so much for failing to reach God's high standards, but for being such fools as to reject his remedy.

"Ah," we can almost hear the Athenians saying, "but who can believe in judgment these days?" Paul had his answer ready. He continued, "Of this he has given assurance to all men by raising him from the dead." His argument is very clear. The judgment is as certain as the resurrection. The resurrection, improbable as it might have seemed, took place in the past. The judgment, improbable as it might seem, will take place in the future. Paul argues from a past certainty to a future one. The resurrection is certain; the judgment is certain. And because nobody can evade it, God commands all men everywhere to repent and entrust themselves to the one who can enable them to face it undismayed.

"All men everywhere." That is comprehensive. The resurrection is addressed to all men everywhere. It speaks to the uninformed, the man or woman who, like the Athenians, had never looked into this sort of thing before. It presents them with clear evidence that there is a God, that in Jesus Christ he has come to us, has died for our sins, and confronts us as the conqueror of death. The resurrection has always been the clearest evidence for the honest inquirer to grapple with.

The resurrection speaks also to the fearful: the person who knows quite well that the Christian story is true, but can't face up to what it will cost. Jesus, the risen one, comes alongside and says, "It is I, do not be afraid." Is it the fear of what friends will say if you change sides? Is it the fear that you will not be able to keep it up? Is it the fear that he will take from you some pleasures you are most reluctant to release, or make impossible demands upon you? He understands those fears. All his first followers had them too, when he met them after the resurrection. They found, and you will find, that there is one force in the world stronger than fear. It is love. "Perfect love casts out fear," said John from experience (1 John 4:18). And once you allow his perfect love to touch you, your fear will melt away.

"All men everywhere." That includes the doubters. God has been very gracious to the doubter. He has provided strong, palpable evidence through the resurrection of Jesus Christ from the dead. That evidence is more than sufficient to warrant belief. We have examined it together. But it will only become *decisive* for you once you take the plunge of commitment to this Jesus. Then you will not just know about him. You will begin to know him. Many a person has come to Christ full of doubts and hesitations, saying in effect, "Lord, I believe; help my unbelief," and has found that even so hesitant a faith, provided it is placed in Christ, opens the door to genuine Christian life and assurance.

"All men everywhere." That includes the apathetic, the person who likes dabbling in religion, or is out for any new experience provided it does not involve commitment. I am sorry, but you cannot come to Christ like that. He is not a pleasant diversion. He is not an aspect of religious experience. He is the one who rose from the dead. He is the one who will judge mankind—judge even you—at the end. There will be no playing around then. We shall have to live with the decisions we have made and the character that has emerged from those decisions. He commands all men everywhere to repent.

Meeting the Resurrected Christ

Very well, you say. I believe Christ rose from the dead. I want to get in touch with him, but how do I actually begin?

It is very simple, as are most of the really important

112

things in life. If you are in earnest, you can start today. I suggest you get alone, or maybe find a friend who is already a Christian, and get on your knees and pray some prayer such as this:

"Lord Jesus Christ, I believe that you came to this earth for the likes of me. I believe you died on the cross to deal with my alienation from God. I believe you rose from the dead and are alive for evermore. Lord, I have kept you out of my life for too long. I realize it will be costly to follow you. I realize there will be a lot of spring cleaning for you to do. I am ready for that, so far as I know. Please come and share my life with me. And make good that promise you gave to your first followers, 'Lo, I am with you always.'"

Or, if you prefer, something even shorter. When Thomas was persuaded that Jesus was alive and was beckoning to him, he simply fell at the feet of the Master and said, "My Lord and my God!" (John 20:28). That was as profound an act of commitment as it was possible to make. And Jesus accepted him. He will do the same for you.

Did he not say, "Him who comes to me I will not cast out"? Learn that verse. You will need it, because you will assuredly be tempted to doubt in the early days of your discipleship. It comes in John 6:37. Learn it by heart, and when doubt strikes, use that promise to repel it. Or this one: "this is the testimony, that God gave us eternal life, and this life is in his Son. He who has the Son has life; he who has not the Son of God has not life" (1 John 5:11-12). What a magnificent

113

black-and-white promise to claim!

Maybe you still feel uncertain. Perhaps you fear you might not do it right, or that you do not know enough of him to take that plunge with confidence. I wonder if this will help you?

Just recently a husband and wife came to see me during a mission in which I was involved. The wife entrusted her life to Christ, much as I have suggested before. The husband went away to think about it. He returned on the last night of the mission. "Michael," he said, "I haven't got there yet." He was a really honest person. So I said to him, "Why don't you pray a simple prayer entrusting as much of yourself as you are aware of to as much of Jesus as you know?" He did so, and almost immediately the joy of making contact with the risen Christ began to fill him. You see, it is not the amount of faith we have that is important, but where that faith is placed. Even slight and doubting faith, if it is put in the risen Jesus, enables his life to begin flowing into ours.

Knowing Christ Better
Well, suppose we take that step. What next?

Let us see what the earliest disciples did in order to develop their own knowledge of the risen Jesus. I think they might give us some advice such as this on the basis of their own experience of Jesus subsequent to Easter day.

Meet the Master. They did, and each time it brought joy and encouragement.

114

Prayer is the way we meet him—prayer at any moment in the day—brief, informal, natural. Though prayer was probably a last resort before we entrusted our lives to him, it begins to become as normal as breathing to the Christian. The barrier of alienation has gone down. We are in touch now, and it is a growing joy to share experiences with him, just as two friends would on a long walk.

Join the community. Isolated Christians are an anomaly. We need the community and the community needs us. Thomas missed the blessing of Christ's appearance on the first Easter evening because he was not with the others—for what reason we do not know (John 20:24). No wonder the writer to the Hebrews warns us not to neglect to meet together, but to encourage one another (Hebrews 10:25). Even if you feel the church in your area is not very exciting, it is most important to get identified with it. Isolated Christians are easy meat for Satan.

Read the book. The two disciples walking to Emmaus on the first Easter day had a wonderful experience from the stranger whom they later realized was the risen Jesus. "Beginning with Moses and all the prophets, he interpreted to them in all the scriptures the things concerning himself." And their response was characteristic of Christians ever since: "They said to each other, 'Did not our hearts burn within us while he talked to us on the road, while he opened to us the scriptures?' " (Luke 24:27, 32).

Regular reading of the Bible is as important to

115

spiritual growth as regular meals are to physical development. If you go short on this you will become a dwarf—or starve. It is as critical as that. And if you think that it is all a bit of a chore, you are wrong. The Bible will become your favorite book because in it you will meet afresh with Jesus Christ and your heart too will burn within you as he opens to you the Scriptures and makes them come alive.

Eat the meal. It was not only the Scriptures that thrilled the hearts of those two disciples on the road. It was also the meal with Jesus. "When he was at table with them, he took the bread and blessed, and broke it, and gave it to them. And their eyes were opened and they recognized him" (Luke 24:30-31).

Throughout the centuries, Christians of every tradition and nationality have found the same. He *does* meet us in the breaking of the bread. He feeds us and we recognize him as we gather round the Lord's table. The Holy Communion is one of the main ways of growing in the knowledge of Jesus. If you mean to develop the relationship, make sure you attend the meal.

Live the life. As a member of the "community of the resurrection" your life will be different from what it used to be. We come to Jesus just as we are, but he does not leave us unchanged. He gets to work on us. That is why there is so much teaching in the epistles of the New Testament on practical Christian behavior—not, mark you, aping the Christians around you. They may have it wrong, in part at least. But it is a matter of seeking to please Christ in all we do. Provided we

116

keep close to him in the ways already indicated, a lot of this change will come imperceptibly. The New Testament says that changed character is not something we work up, but fruit which the Holy Spirit produces in our lives once we give him access: "love, joy, peace, patience, kindness, goodness, faithfulness, gentleness, self-control" (Galatians 5:22-23). This is the fruit that grows in Christian lives.

Use the power. He has the strength you need for living the Christian life. You don't. Therefore, from the very outset you must start turning to Christ and claiming his power in your temptations, in your moods of depression, in your loneliness and in your failures.

There is an enemy of souls, as you will very quickly discover if you haven't already. And his strategy is not to encourage you to commit terrible sins; it is much simpler than that. He wants to keep you out of touch with Jesus Christ. Therefore your prayer life will be attacked. So will your church going, so will your Bible reading. He is out to distance you from Jesus your Lord. If he can achieve that, he will be satisfied. So if you want to make a success of the Christian life, make sure that you keep close to Christ. For the Christian life begins when you put your life in the hands of the risen Lord, and it grows riper every day as you keep your life in those hands.

Christ's Transforming Power
Here is a concrete illustration of that transforming power of Jesus. Fred is a cockney. He was, as he him-

self put it, "an embryo gangster, already with a list of crimes which society could level against me, and sins which accuse me of their own accord." The story of Fred's conversion (in a big rally he attended on a dare to meet a girl!) is fascinating enough, but the sequel is more interesting still. He is now an Army chaplain. This is what he has to say about the revolution that has made him the man he is:

The living Christ has given me what no court, no psychiatrist, no probation officer could give me—the consciousness of sins forgiven. The living Christ has given me a sense that he understands and cares for me, which no other friendship has ever fulfilled. This alone has been of enormous therapeutic value to my scarred soul.

The proof of the pudding is in the eating. The proof of a living Christ lies in a personal relationship with him. My experience of him since my conversion has been varied, and with trials enough to make me very sure of him. Army life, on active service with the Parachute Brigade in various parts of the world, has removed the possibility of my faith being due to weak sentimentality. The harsh reality of fighting the continually exposed weaknesses in my own character (in particular, refusal to acknowledge my limitations, coupled with smugness and self-assertion) have dismissed the possibility of my experience being merely emotional. Emotion does not sustain the continuing effort needed to suppress the passions which war against the soul.

The personal discipline that education and char-acter-training have demanded of me is not likely to have sprung from wishful thinking! The joy of a loving wife, two children and a happy and secure home, have shown me that through the living Christ even one who, like myself, was once described by a magistrate as a "social menace" can be more than just tolerable. That is something of the difference that Jesus Christ has made, and continues to make to me.

Such is the testimony of one of the most complete men's men I have ever met: paratrooper, footballer for the Army and Brighton, boxing champion, and so on. All Fred's potential gangsterlike characteristics have been taken over, redirected, and harnessed by Jesus Christ. That is what the risen Lord can do in any one of us once he is invited to take over. What other power is there in the world that can do the same?

Let's end with the three questions with which this book began.

What is life all about? The purpose of life is to know the Lord and to enjoy him forever.

What is the supreme need of our society? To be recon-ciled with the Jesus who died for us and rose again. Once in touch with him, each of us can become what we are meant to be in society: "light" and "salt" was how Jesus put it.

Is there a life beyond the grave? Indeed there is, and that has been crystal clear since the day death died.

Don't miss it.

Bibliography

Anderson, Norman. *Evidence for the Resurrection*. Downers Grove, Ill.: InterVarsity Press, 1966.

Lewis, C. S. *Miracles*. New York: Macmillan, 1963.

Morison, Frank. *Who Moved the Stone?* Downers Grove, Ill.: InterVarsity Press, 1958.

Ramsey, A. M. *The Resurrection of Christ*. London: Bles, 1945.

Schonfield, Hugh. *The Passover Plot*. New York: Bantam, 1971.

Weatherhead, Leslie. *The Resurrection of Christ*. London: Hodder and Stoughton, 1959.